Enjoying Big Bend National Park

Rufous hummingbird

Number Forty-one:
W. L. Moody Jr. Natural History Series

ATM travel guides

Enjoying

Texas A&M University Press

College Station

Big Bend National Park

A Friendly Guide to Adventures for Everyone

By Gary Clark

Photographs by Kathy Adams Clark

This paper meets the requirements of ANSI/NISO Z39.48-1992
(Permanence of Paper).
Binding materials have been chosen for durability.

Library of Congress Cataloging-in-Publication Data

Clark, Gary, 1943–
  Enjoying Big Bend National Park : a friendly guide to adventures
for everyone / by Gary Clark ; photographs by Kathy Adams Clark. — 1st ed.
     p. cm. — (W. L. Moody Jr. natural history series ; no. 41)
  Includes index.
  ISBN-13: 978-1-60344-101-8 (flexbound : alk. paper)
  ISBN-10: 1-60344-101-8 (flexbound : alk. paper)
   1. Big Bend National Park (Tex.)—Guidebooks.   2. Hiking—Texas—
Big Bend National Park—Guidebooks.   3. Automobile travel—Texas—
Big Bend National Park—Guidebooks. 4. Nature observation—Texas—
Big Bend National Park—Guidebooks.   I. Clark, Kathy Adams, 1955–
II. Title.   III. Series.
F392.B53C58   2009
917.964'9320464—dc22
2008036919

Contents

Adventures for the Physically Fit

Adventures at an Easy Pace

Adventures for People with Limited Physical Mobility

Adventures in a Vehicle

Adventures for Nature Lovers

Preface

ALMOST every year for twenty-five years, I have visited Big Bend National Park at the U-shaped bend in the Rio Grande of southwest Texas. You would think after so many visits I would find few adventures left in the park. Not so.

I have hiked the mountain and desert trails, camped in the primitive backcountry, driven over the fearsomely rugged back roads, and crossed the Rio Grande into the Mexican border towns (in the days before the border at Big Bend was closed). I have luxuriated in the Chisos Mountains Lodge and dined in its restaurant overlooking an inexpressibly beautiful mountain valley.

There is no regularly occurring bird in Big Bend I haven't seen, nor have I missed many of the rare birds of Big Bend. I have watched my wife photograph untold numbers of butterflies that rival the desert wildflowers with their dramatic colors and have come face to face with a black bear, had a mountain lion stare at me, watched Carmen white-tailed deer graze peacefully in mountain meadows, and laughed at striped skunks chasing gray foxes. Oh, yes, I have also seen western diamondback rattlesnakes measuring six feet long and as big around as an ax handle.

Yet I still feel a sense of adventure every time I enter the park, even after so many years. The park continues to surprise me with spectacular events like the powerful waterfalls that occurred during an unusual season of strong rains. I still discover new plants and new creatures, and my every visit swells my knowledge of the flora and fauna that live in the park.

The park is a kaleidoscope of wilderness scenes, always shifting into symmetries of color and shape mingled with stunning views of wild creatures and wildflowers. No two days in the park are ever the same. Surprising sights are the order of the day, every day.

Big Bend is a rugged, remote place, isolated from any sizable town by a hundred miles. Neither cell phones nor pagers work out there (although that may change, soon). For now, the only reliable way to call out is to use a pay phone at the ranger headquarters. Not even motel rooms and cabins at the Chisos Mountains Lodge in the Basin have telephones—or television. The park has no swimming pools, no tennis courts, and no golf courses. Unlike many other national parks, Big Bend National Park has no city-type entertainment for visitors. It is a one-of-a-kind wilderness, and you take it or leave it on its own terms.

Nonetheless, I want everyone, regardless of his or her enthusiasm for the outdoors, to experience the park. The rooms at the lodge are comfortable enough for the most tender footed among us. The reconnection people get with nature in Big Bend—America's last frontier wilderness—is worth at least a day or two of disconnection with urban life.

The park is breathtakingly beautiful. It is a vast area covering over 800,000 acres, slightly larger than Yosemite National Park. The Chisos Mountains in the center of the park rise nearly 8,000 feet from the sprawling and uncommonly verdant Chihuahuan Desert. The park contains diverse ecological systems from cool mountain forests to steamy, hot river floodplains.

Birds are abundant, and every summer I watch them. I always take a hike to Boot Canyon in the high Chisos Mountains to see the Colima warbler, the signature bird of the park. It migrates to the park from Mexico to breed during spring and summer in the cool, moist mountain canyons decorated with pinyon pines, madrone trees, oaks, and bigtooth maples. I also reacquaint myself with other birds like the subtly hued varied bunting, the uncommon hepatic tanager, the sprightly plumed Scott's oriole, the secretive gray vireo, and the tiny but gorgeous Lucifer hummingbird. I search out the usual birds like crissal thrasher, pyrrhuloxia, verdin, and Bell's vireo as well as rare birds like tropical kingbird and black hawk. While looking for a black hawk one year, I spotted a mountain lion fifty yards in front of me patrolling the edge of the riparian brushland.

My wife, Kathy, stalks Big Bend for butterflies. Big Bend hosts a mind-boggling variety of butterflies, many of which are still being cataloged. Kathy looks for butterflies like the Palmer's metalmark with its beautiful orange, tan, and white wings; the red-spotted purple with its large black wings sporting bright red spots; and the California sister—my favorite—with large brown wings chalked by twin white bands. Several times, we have taken our son, Michael, and his children, Nicholas and Bethany, to Big Bend. Nicholas developed a passion for birds while visiting the park one year. I helped him track down his first elf owl, the smallest owl in North America. He jumped up and down like a typical avid birder with the thrill of a great new bird added to his life list.

Bethany enjoyed the mammals. We once sat with her quietly at dusk and watched a group of gray foxes forage in the Chisos Basin. Ambling nearby was a striped skunk, which Bethany named Mr. Stinky. To this day, every skunk we see gets the moniker "Mr. Stinky."

My son has enjoyed the rocks from the first time I took him to the park so long ago. I remember him as a little boy being fascinated with rugged mountains formed from lava of ancient volcanoes and with cliffs

Striped skunk

at river canyons formed from stratified layers of ancient limestone. Not surprisingly, he became a geologist.

I'm sure many a scientist can trace a career back to inspirations at Big Bend. But all of us—children and adults—can draw inspirations for the ordinary business of living from extraordinary experiences in Big Bend.

Kathy and I always have a magnificent time in the park from the moment we arrive to the day we leave. One year when we were driving out, we saw a black bear strolling on the Chisos Basin Road and a peregrine falcon soaring over Panther Junction. Then we saw a family of scaled quail with tiny chicks scurrying along the desert. Coming or going, we've found that every day holds adventures in Big Bend National Park, and in this book, we will help you discover and enjoy the park's bounty of adventures.

Preface

Southwestern earless lizard

Enjoying Big Bend National Park

Engelmann's prickly-pear

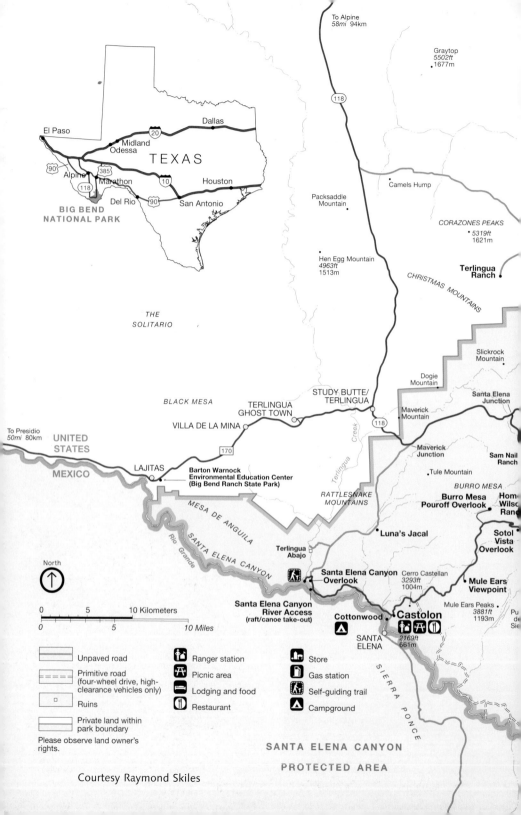

To Alpine
58mi 94km

Graytop
5502ft
1677m

(118)

TEXAS

El Paso

Dallas

Midland
Odessa

20

T E X A S

90

385

Alpine
118

10

Houston

Marathon

Del Rio

90

San Antonio

BIG BEND
NATIONAL PARK

Camels Hump

Packsaddle
Mountain

CORAZONES PEAKS

5319ft
1621m

Hen Egg Mountain
4963ft
1513m

CHRISTMAS MOUNTAINS

Terlingua
Ranch

THE
SOLITARIO

Slickrock
Mountain

Dogie
Mountain

Santa Elena
Junction

BLACK MESA

TERLINGUA
GHOST TOWN

STUDY BUTTE/
TERLINGUA

118

Maverick
Mountain

VILLA DE LA MINA

Maverick
Junction

Sam Nail
Ranch

To Presidio
50mi 80km

UNITED
STATES

170

Tule Mountain

BURRO MESA

MEXICO

LAJITAS

Barton Warnock
Environmental Education Center
(Big Bend Ranch State Park)

RATTLESNAKE
MOUNTAINS

Burro Mesa
Pouroff Overlook

Hom
Wils
Ran

MESA DE ANGUILA

Luna's Jacal

Sotol
Vista
Overlook

Terlingua
Abajo

Santa Elena Canyon
Overlook

Cerro Castellan
3293ft
1004m

Mule Ears
Viewpoint

North

SANTA ELENA CANYON

Santa Elena Canyon
River Access
(raft/canoe take-out)

Cottonwood

Castolon

Mule Ears Peaks
3881ft
1193m

Pu
de
Sie

0   5   10 Kilometers

0   5   10 Miles

Rio Grande

SANTA
ELENA

2169ft
661m

SIERRA

Unpaved road

Primitive road
(four-wheel drive, high-
clearance vehicles only)

Ruins

Private land within
park boundary

Please observe land owner's
rights.

Ranger station

Picnic area

Lodging and food

Restaurant

Store

Gas station

Self-guiding trail

Campground

PONCE

SANTA ELENA CANYON

PROTECTED AREA

Courtesy Raymond Skiles

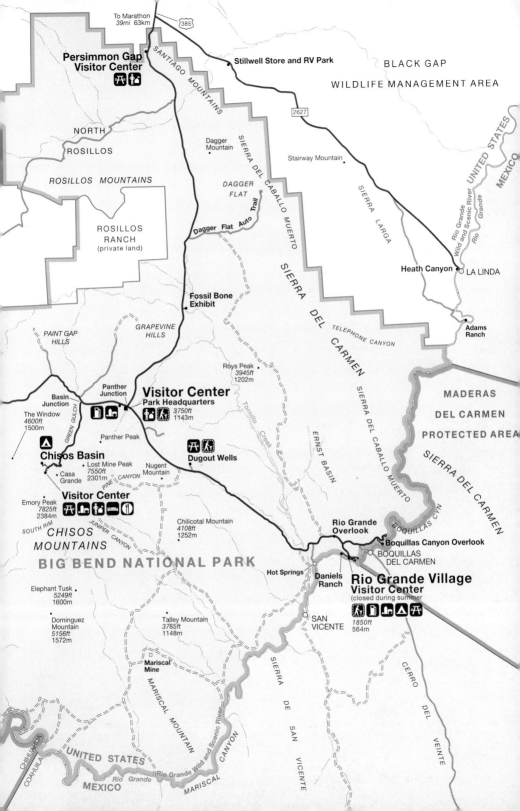

Two-tailed swallowtail

The Lure of Big Bend

I WILL never forget the first time I drove to Big Bend National Park. It was late afternoon, and I had driven there with my eleven-year-old son from a cabin we had rented in the summer of 1975 on the Frio River near Concan, Texas. I had planned to drive to Big Bend, spend a few hours, and drive back—grossly underestimating the distance and drive time. Like many Texans, I had looked at the park on the map a zillion times but never had taken time to visit. I wasn't bored in the Frio River country, and the sole reason for an excursion to Big Bend was a need to satisfy my curiosity about an area of Texas I had never seen.

As soon as I entered the small town of Sanderson on U.S. Highway 90, I realized I was entering a world wholly unlike anything I had ever seen before. A mountainous desert, yes, but nothing like similar places I had visited in New Mexico or Arizona. Something about the land sent a shiver up my spine, not of fear but of anticipation.

When my car turned down Highway 385 from Marathon toward the Big Bend, my eyes widened in wonder as if I were headed for a different planet. The closer I came to the Big Bend mountain range, the more I was certain I was no longer on Earth.

"Michael," I said to my son, who was a fan of the TV series *Star Trek*, "I believe we're going where no man has gone before."

By the time the Chisos Mountains came into view, I was stunned, overcome by the feeling that I had discovered a preternatural world. My son was as wide-eyed as I was. We were both speechless. The boy inside me was too overwhelmed to speak, and the boy sitting beside me was too awed to talk.

I drove the car onto the Chisos Basin Road, winding up into what looked like the ancient kingdom of a long-lost civilization, with a naturally carved castle at the top—Casa Grande. Tall, statuesque, rock-hewn pillars stood among the mountains like the weather-beaten icons of Easter Island. The road wound up and then down slightly into a luminously green basin rimmed by imposing, craggy mountains. By now, my son and I were hardly silent. We were whooping with joy.

We ate dinner at the lodge and watched the sun set radiantly as if by magic in the center of a V-shaped gouge at the western end of the mountain rim, a formation I later learned was called the Window. We rented a little clapboard cabin, more like a hut, and slept uneasily as a violent thunderstorm roared over the mountains. Next morning, we headed up the Pinnacles Trail, intent on making it to the park's highest peak on Mount Emory.

But I was no hiker in those days. Didn't know about taking water. Didn't know about wearing sturdy hiking boots. Just wanted to trek as fast as I could with my son to the top of the mountain. Didn't occur to me that there would be no running stream where we could slurp down water as we did in the Frio River country. Amazingly, we both made it to the rim of the Pinnacles, a good 2-mile ascent to about 7,000 feet.

Hot Springs complex

But dire thirst made us abandon our goal of reaching the mountaintop. We raced back down to the Basin, went to the store by the lodge, bought four or five six-packs of Dr. Pepper, and downed them in 15 minutes. The experience taught me a life-altering lesson. Never go anywhere in Big Bend without water.

Keeping to that lesson, I have enjoyed a lifetime of adventures in Big Bend, some with my son, some alone, and most with my wife, Kathy. She and I have also led tours to Big Bend and watched as people's eyes widened in wonder as mine did so long ago—and still do. Whether driving the roads of Big Bend to look at the scenery or walking the trails to feel the rocks beneath my feet, I have never failed to quench my thirst for adventure.

Big Bend Rocks

According to Indian legend, when the Great Creator made the Earth and had finished placing the stars in the sky, the birds in the air, and the fish in the sea, there was a large pile of rejected stony materials left over. He threw this material into one heap and made the Big Bend.

—Ross A. Maxwell, *The Big Bend of the Rio Grande*

Big Bend is about rocks. Giant pillars made from rocks, mountains hoisted out of rocks, deserts strewn with rocks, and river bends cutting through canyons of rocks. Some of the rocks were born at the birth of the North American continent, some during warps in the earth as tectonic plates shifted position, and some from lava extrusions of horrendous volcanoes. However formed, Big Bend's rocks present a giant jigsaw puzzle of daunting complexity that geologists have yet to fully piece together.

I am no geologist. But Kathy and my geologist son, Michael, are dedicated students of Big Bend rocks. From their explanations, I can visualize a rough geologic history in the rock formations as I hike and drive around the park, although I admit that Ross Maxwell's Indian legend telling how Big Bend was formed fits my brain just fine.

Tuff Canyon

What strikes me most about the geology of Big Bend is the tremendous stretches of time during which the land formed, changed, and formed again. For instance, when I drive into the park at Persimmon Gap, I see remnants of rocks from the Paleozoic era some 500 million years ago. I discovered that those Paleozoic rocks were actually heaved up by the 300-million-year-old Ouachita mountain-building episode caused by buckling of the southeastern North American continent as the South American oceanic plate crushed into it.

Before the Ouachita episode, a deep oceanic basin covered Big Bend for over 300 million years during the Paleozoic era; following the Ouachita event and subsequent erosion, a shallow sea called the Sundance Sea covered the land during the Cretaceous period about 135 million years ago. The sea left deposits of limestone that I can see as stratified layers in the 1,500-foot walls of Santa Elena Canyon. The sea also left behind the fossilized remains of marine animals that my son and wife eagerly point out at Boquillas Canyon.

A second mountain-building event called the Laramide orogeny came near the end of the Cretaceous period about 65 million years ago when the Rocky Mountains were generated from ancient sediments shoved up by a scrunching of the earth's crust. The southernmost exposure of the U.S. Rockies lies at Mariscal Mountain in Big Bend.

The scene that most interests me, though, is Pine Canyon in the Chisos Mountains, shaped by hellish volcanic activity some 35 million years ago that shot up massive extrusions of lava to mold much of the profile of the Chisos. A stunning example of that profile is Casa Grande, a mountainous rectangular block standing like a sixteenth-century Irish castle on the eastern side of the Chisos Basin. Casa Grande is solidified lava atop a bed of volcanic strata born out of a cataclysmic eruption in the earth. Look in awe, as I do, at the rocks and mountains of Big Bend, for awesome forces sculpted the unparalleled beauty of this landscape.

Big Bend's Human Culture

Nowhere do I hike or drive in Big Bend without being aware that people have lived among the prodigious mountains and vast deserts for thousands of years. Beginning with Paleo-Indians ten thousand years

Silhouette of Chisos Mountains

ago, humans have eked out a living by foraging, hunting, farming, or ranching in the formidable terrain. Evidence of longtime human habitation exists in the form of metates milled into rocky plateaus above Rio Grande Village by ancient Native American peoples; in the form of arrowheads, perhaps hammered out by Native Americans such as the Chisos, Mescalero Apaches, and Comanches; in the form of still-standing adobe homes used by Mexican farmers; in the form of remnant corrals where ranchers kept horses; in the form of a rock-hewn post office that was the center of an early twentieth-century resort at Hot Springs; and in the form of a grave just north of Panther Junction along the highway to Marathon with this epitaph on the tombstone:

> *Nina Seawall Hannold*
> *August 26, 1880*
> *Sept 30, 1911*

Enjoying Big Bend National Park

Nina Hannold's husband, Curtis, was a schoolteacher who traveled by either horseback or maybe buckboard 8 miles east to the schoolhouse at Dugout Wells. His young bride, whom he had brought to Big Bend from Oklahoma by covered wagon in 1908, often sat reading to her children near her home by a spring-fed stream—now called Hannold's Draw—under the cool shade of cottonwood trees. I have often pictured Nina looking up from a book and gazing at the surreal profile of the Chisos Mountains to the south. Did she ever get up to the Chisos Basin and gaze at the Window? I do not know. I do know she died during pregnancy after residing with her husband three brief years at what must have been in her time a blissful oasis near Panther Junction.

Over at Sam Nail's Ranch on the western side of the park at the base of Burro Mesa, I can stand next to the remaining adobe wall of the ranch home that Sam and his brother, Jim, built in 1916. After marrying Nena Burnam in 1918, Sam continued to work the homestead of milk cows, chickens, cattle, fruit trees, and a garden. I like to picture Sam waking up at daybreak one spring morning in 1920 to glance at the V-shaped slice on the western face of the Chisos Mountains that would later be dubbed the Window. His homestead was an oasis, fed by spring water that he pulled up with a windmill. Songbirds filled the canopy of cottonwood trees, as they do today, and I imagine the dawn chorus of birds was Sam's wake-up call every morning as he rose to begin the hard task of ranching on an unforgiving land.

But nothing intrigues me more than the metates, the cylindrical holes—some the size of a coffee cup, others the size of a bucket—ground into limestone ledges above the river at Rio Grande Village and Boquillas Canyon. The holes were cooking apparatuses devised by ancient Native Americans to grind mesquite seeds into a flourlike substance as a basis for meals or maybe to mash edible fruits into a kind of tasty dessert. The metates tell of communities that lived on the hills overlooking the Rio Grande. Surely, community denizens raised families, taught children to hunt and fish, had festivals to celebrate seasonal changes, told tales of heroism in the days of their ancestors, defended their communities against attack by enemies, mourned the deaths of stillborn babies and aged grandfathers, and enjoyed quiet walks by the river as the setting sun cast the desert and mountainsides in a vivid hue of orange.

Chisos Hedgehog

Black Bears

Nothing will shoot adrenaline through your body like standing face-to-face with a 6-foot, 400-pound black bear. I had the experience by happenstance one day while hiking the high Chisos Mountains. Being most respectful of the magnificent beast and knowing that one swipe of its paw across my face could end my days upon this earth, I screamed and waved my arms. I knew that unlike brown bears and grizzly bears, black bears are fearful of humans and generally run away from them, unless, of course, people try to offer the bears food. I wasn't about to offer a snack bar to the burly creature at my face, and I was glad to let it run off in fear of my yells and gesticulating arms.

I remember when black bears returned to Big Bend in the late 1980s after a long hiatus. Way before my time, the bears had roamed commonly throughout the Big Bend region. But trapping and hunting as well as the clearing of land for ranching had driven the bears completely out of Big Bend by the time the national park was established in 1944. People would spot a bear in the park on rare occasions, but no resident bears existed until the late twentieth century.

The return of black bears to Big Bend may be the first time a species of large mammal that was extirpated from a region has recolonized that region without human assistance. Wildlife scientists believe the repopulation in Big Bend started with a female (called a sow) that came up from the Sierra del Carmen range in Mexico near the southeastern border of the park. Perhaps a sow with cubs crossed the Rio Grande, strolled across the desert, and wandered into the cool forests of the Chisos Mountains. She probably mated with a male (called a boar) that had also wandered into the mountains, thereby beginning an increase in resident black bears.

However, the black bear population in Big Bend has waned a bit since 2000, although the reason for the decline is unclear. Maybe the long drought of the 1990s, maybe a normal return to the mountains of Mexico, or maybe a retreat from a park that sometimes overflows with visitors drove off many of the bears. Anyway, the chances of seeing a bear are slimmer now than when I came eyeball to eyeball with the big beast. Yet chances may improve. Bears still roam the park, and the park service maintains habitat conducive to bear conservation.

No need to fear bears, but do understand their behavior. Bears can sniff odors a mile away. They are enticed by food of all sorts and by smelly stuff like toothpaste. Therefore, if you camp, hike, or picnic in the park, store your food and toiletries in bear-proof containers, and use the bear-proof storage lockers at backpacking campsites and camp-grounds. Throw your trash in bear-proof trash dumpsters located in all areas of the park.

Remember, I did not intentionally walk up to a bear in the high mountains—never would. I respect black bears as big, powerful, and wonderfully wild beasts that I know will leave me alone if I leave them alone. And if I leave them be, hopefully they will reestablish a perma-nent home in America's last frontier at Big Bend National Park.

Birder of the Big Bend

I'm a birder—a longtime, dedicated, and at times obsessive birder. Wherever I travel, whether in the States, Canada, Europe, or Central America, the first question I ask is, "What birds will I see?"

When I first asked that question about Big Bend, I was overwhelmed. A park with a list of over four hundred birds, two-thirds the number of birds recorded in all of Texas and more birds by far than I would find in any other national park. Of course, I knew I wouldn't see all the species in one trip, nor in several trips, because many of them were migratory and some had been seen only occasionally. But the park was a paradise of birds, and I was set on seeing as many as possible.

I immediately bought a copy of *A Field Guide to the Birds of Big Bend*, by Roland Wauer, a former park naturalist whom I had the plea-sure of interviewing not long ago for my *Houston Chronicle* newspaper column. I read his book cover to cover, in one sitting, absorbing as much as I could from the book's wealth of information about which birds showed up in what areas of the park and in which seasons of the year.

But the bird that immediately captured my fancy was the Colima warbler, which nests during spring and summer in the high Chisos Mountains in Boot Canyon. For years, birders thought the little warbler from Mexico came only to the Chisos to nest; but recently, birders have

California Sister

discovered nesting birds at Mount Livermore near Fort Davis some 130 miles to the north. Boot Canyon, though, remains the only place most people can go to see the bird in North America.

It took me a couple of summers of trudging up to Boot Canyon to see the bird because, for a time, I could only take vacations in August when most of the Colimas had already migrated back to Mexico. Then came the year I went to the park in early summer. I rolled out of bed at dawn one morning and headed up the knee-crunching Pinnacles Trail and ultimately down the Boot Canyon Trail, altogether a lung-taxing 4.5-mile hike. No sooner had I rounded the bend to Boot Springs, the epicenter of Boot Canyon, than I saw several park rangers and a host of guys standing like sentries and wearing dark sunglasses, a distinctly odd thing to wear on this overcast day. Upon seeing pack mules in the corral by the ranger cabin, I knew the fellows had made their way up the mountain the easy way.

A park ranger walked up to me, greeted me with the kindest of smiles, and said, "You must be looking for the Colima." No doubt, he had discerned my intention because of the binoculars around my neck.

"Sure am," I said. "Has anyone seen it this morning?"

"Not yet," he replied. "But if you'd like to join us, you're welcome. We're helping Secretary James Schlesinger get the bird for his life list."

My jaw dropped. I knew the then secretary of energy under President Carter was a birder but never dreamed I'd be birding with him. Yet minutes later, there I was birding right beside him, surrounded by what I presumed were secret service agents. Schlesinger greeted me most graciously, smiling a wry kind of smile, and nodding his head covered in a mane of whitish hair.

"I think I hear the bird," he whispered.

"Me, too," I gulped.

A park ranger yelled, "There it is!"

But Schlesinger quickly replied, "No, that's a Hutton's vireo."

Then, a small bird flitted through the oaks lining the creek at Boot Canyon, and Schlesinger called out in a stentorian voice, "Colima, Colima, Colima!"

"Is that a lifer for you, too?" he asked.

"Oh, yes," I said.

He shook my hand in congratulations as all good birders do upon getting a life bird.

Since that momentous sighting of a Colima warbler some thirty years ago, I have never failed to find the bird on my spring or summer hikes to Boot Canyon. And every time I see it, I can hear Schlesinger's booming voice saying, "Colima, Colima, Colima!"

Butterfly-Styled Hiking

For most of my life, my style of hiking was to make a beeline to a destination. If I was headed up to Boot Canyon in the high Chisos Mountains, I went straight up the Pinnacles Trail as fast as possible because it was the shortest route. If I wanted to hike to the Window Trail, my idea was to get to the pour-off at the base of the Window as quickly as my feet would take me. No dawdling, no stopping to look at a flower or tree, not even a bird unless it was one I had never seen before. Hiking was like a race to a finish line, and I was a fabulously fast hiker.

Sightseeing for me was at the destination—a canyon, a mountaintop, a mountain rim, a peculiar rock formation in the middle of the desert, or a waterfall tucked in a mountainside. Nothing along the trail was worth stopping to see. The trail was a means to an end, and the end was what mattered.

My wife, Kathy, had a wholly different style of hiking, one I dubbed "butterfly hiking." She would zigzag languidly like a butterfly all over the trail, stopping here and there to look at a bug, smell a flower, examine a rock, or feel the texture of a tree leaf between her fingers. As a professional nature photographer, she would also snap a picture of . . . well . . . everything. Drove me nuts. But I would always wait patiently—okay, impatiently—for her to catch up with me at the end of the trail.

One day on a hike down the Window Trail, I indulged her by strolling beside her in the "butterfly hiking" technique. Or maybe she indulged me. Anyway, what I came to realize was that I had been a numbskull hiker for years, passing up exquisite beauties of nature in senseless haste down a trail.

Kathy had been the smarter hiker all along. She would study the oblong leaf shape of a Gray's oak and rub her hand over the leaf's sandpaper-like surface. She would examine tracks in the mud along the trail, often discerning paw prints of a mountain lion. No butterfly escaped her glance, and she would take stunning pictures of butterflies like California sisters and empress leilias. She would bend over to cup her fingers around a flower like an Apache plume, a showy white flower that produces a feathery fruit. Rock outcrops that were obstacles to me would rivet her attention. While I whizzed past a common bird, like a cactus wren, she would stop to find its nest, a ball of grass and twigs stuck snuggly in the middle of a cholla cactus or yucca tree.

By the time Kathy reached the end of a trail, she had already enjoyed a glorious adventure by opening her senses to Big Bend's spectacular array of natural treasures. While I hiked like a marathon runner, she hiked like an archeologist, relishing every scrap of life and every shard of rock along the trail.

I've been a "butterfly hiker" ever since that day I deigned to walk at my wife's pace. I learned a lesson not only about hiking in Big Bend but also about living life: most of us spend too much energy rushing to the end of the trail, rarely pausing to savor what is on it.

Practical Information about Visiting Big Bend

DRINK WATER! DRINK WATER! DRINK WATER!

■ The dry air in a desert environment causes moisture in your body to evaporate more quickly than you may realize. This is apparent when you see that perspiration dries within minutes. Therefore, rehydrate your body by drinking water about every 15 minutes.

■ **Do not wait until you are thirsty to drink water!** Your body can begin dehydrating without your knowing it, so drink water even when you have no thirst to quench.

■ Each member of your party should always travel with a full water bottle. Adults should carry a 16- or 32-ounce water bottle, and children should have an 8-ounce water bottle at all times.

■ An adult should drink a gallon, or 64 ounces, of water per day, especially in the summer. Never pass up a water spigot or fountain without filling your water containers.

■ Watch your children and elderly members of your party to make sure they are drinking enough water. Sodas and juices do not rehydrate the body as quickly and efficiently as plain water, so make sure everyone is guzzling water.

■ Urinate often. A friend who is an anatomy professor says that an active kidney is a happy kidney. Urination is a good sign that the body is well hydrated. Drink water often and urinate often.

■ If you stop for a salty snack, be sure you drink 8 or more ounces of water. Balance your intake of caffeine and alcohol, both of which are diuretics, with a tall tumbler or bottle of water to keep your body hydrated.

■ Be alert to signs of dehydration, which include headache, fatigue, and irritability. Remember, thirst is not a sign of dehydration. On a desert hike years ago, I almost lost my wife to hyperthermia brought on by dehydration, and she wasn't at all thirsty. The lesson is DRINK WATER! Lots of water.

Equipment List

Hat

A wide-brimmed hat protects your head, neck, and ears from the intense sunlight in the park. In addition, a good hat retains vital moisture around the skull. Baseball hats are fine for walking around campgrounds and amphitheaters, but you would be wise to wear a wide-brimmed hat on an extended hike.

Sunglasses

Sunlight in Big Bend is intensely bright. In such bright light, the iris of the eye closes to block harmful light rays. Once the iris is constricted to its minimum diameter, the eyelids begin squinting to block more light. Damage to the retina follows if the iris cannot block enough light.

Wear sunglasses to protect your eyes. We suggest that you invest in quality sunglasses for all members of your party. People with eye problems or sensitive eyes may want prescription sunglasses. Sunglasses with ultraviolet (UV) protection prevent damage to the cornea and retina. Cheap sunglasses without UV protection allow the iris to open wider but offer no protection to the exposed retina.

Polarized sunglasses block harsh, white, reflected light coming from water and car windshields. They also block glare from rocky surfaces, bird feathers, and leaves, allowing you to see colors otherwise obscured by glaring light.

Sunscreen

Wear sunscreen all through the daylight hours in Big Bend National Park, whether you're in the park winter, spring, summer, or fall. Sunlight in the park is intense, because of the high mountain elevations and because of the reflective surface of the rocks and desert terrain. Wear sunscreen even if you're only going for a short stroll. Without a protective layer of sunscreen, you may find yourself suffering a bit of sunburn in less than an hour's time spent outdoors in the park.

Before leaving your lodge or campsite, smear a layer of sunscreen on any exposed skin. Remember to cover the back of your neck and the top of your ears, two areas that can take a severe beating from the sun. Keep a tube of sunscreen handy in your pocket, daypack, or backpack and apply it often to exposed skin.

Children and people with fair skin should be particularly careful to apply sunscreen frequently to exposed skin.

Years ago, we went hiking with the late David Alloway, an interpretive naturalist at Big Bend Ranch State Park just west of the national park. It was the middle of July with the temperature exceeding 110 degrees Fahrenheit. David, a legendary expert on desert survival (he told us he had trained Navy Seals in desert survival!), was wearing a long-sleeved shirt, long-legged pants, and a broad-rimmed hat in addition to a layer of sunscreen on his arms and face. We dressed like he did and have been doing so ever since on excursions to the Big Bend country.

Hiking Boots

You can get along with athletic shoes or walking shoes if you never leave the pavement or sidewalks. But if you walk the trails, you'll be wise to put a sturdy pair of hiking boots on your feet. Hiking trails are covered in loose rocks that can tear through ordinary shoes.

Wear hiking boots with sturdy soles to protect the bottoms of your feet and with at least ankle-high tops to protect your ankles. Backpacking into the mountains requires heavy-duty hiking boots. Otherwise, lightweight boots will meet your needs on most trails. Whatever the style of your boots, make sure they are waterproof. A sudden rainstorm can turn trails into streams. The last thing you want is water-soaked feet when hiking.

We recommend closed-toed boots rather than hiking sandals for the trails. Closed-toed boots offer protection from jagged rocks and cacti.

Good Socks

Thick hiking socks complement hiking boots. Hiking socks have thicker soles and extra padding around the toes and heels. Many hiking socks use modern technology to wick moisture away from the skin to prevent skin damage on a long hike.

Binoculars

Follow these steps to align binoculars for your eyes:

■ Binoculars should have a central pivot point that allows both barrels to be moved up and down.

■ Hold the binoculars up to your eyes and move both barrels until you see one circle of light. The circle should be edged in black.

■ Set the eyecups. Eyecups should be extended for people without glasses and folded in for people with glasses.

■ Set the diopter. Most binoculars have a little dial situated below one of the ocular lenses or next to the center focusing wheel that allows you to adjust the focusing for your eyes. People with 20/20 vision can usually leave the diopter at zero. Others need to make minor adjustments. Adjust the diopter while you are reading a sign. When the letters become clear, the diopter is set to the correct position.

Compass

A typical compass has a needle with one end painted red and the other end painted black, white, or some other color. A compass also has a compass housing that turns around the needle. The compass housing shows N for north, E for East, S for South, and W for west.

Place the compass on a flat surface or flat in the palm of your hand. Let the needle settle in one place. Turn the compass housing to align the N with the red end of the needle. The needle is now pointing north.

Make sure the flat surface where you place the compass is free of iron that could cause a magnetic attraction to the compass needle and draw it away from north.

Place the compass on top of a map with the map facing north and the compass facing north, and determine the direction you want to go. Check your compass heading every 100 yards or so to make sure you're on course.

Topographic Maps

A topographic map is a flat representation of a three-dimensional surface. Contour lines on the map join points that have the same elevation. For instance, a contour line labeled 500' will connect all the points at the elevation of 500 feet. Contour lines close together show a sharp incline. Lines that are far apart indicate a level terrain.

Hikers use topographic maps to plan routes to their destination and to locate hiking trails. A scale on the map allows you to calculate distance on the map and convert that to distance on the terrain. For instance, a "1:24,000" map would mean "1 inch on the map equals 24,000 inches on the ground." Another scale allows conversion to feet, miles, and meters.

The thirty-one topographic maps for Big Bend National Park are on a scale of 1:24,000 and have contour lines at 40-foot intervals. All are on sale at the Panther Junction Visitor Center and can be ordered online from the U.S. Geological Survey at http://store.usgs.gov/. Backpackers and anyone traveling off the main trails or paved road should carry a topographic map for the areas traveled.

Handheld GPS (Global Positioning System) Units

GPS units are battery-powered computational devices that access a system of satellites called the Global Position System, allowing you to find your location and track your movements anywhere on earth. The units are intuitive to use and display color maps of your location. They also incorporate a compass and altimeter. A GPS unit appropriate for hiking will cost more than two hundred dollars.

If you can afford it, buy a GPS unit that makes orienteering a snap. But we recommend using it in conjunction with a topographic map (plus an old-fashioned compass) when hiking in Big Bend National Park.

Maps

The Park Service provides maps for all areas in the park. Park maps give visitors information about trails, camping areas, and travel routes. Maps are available at the concessions and at Ranger Stations for a nominal fee. Maps are also available in PDF format from the Big Bend National Park website (www.nps.gov/bibe/index.htm) under the heading "Plan Your Visit."

Field Guides

Field guides are available to help with identification of critters in Big Bend National Park. We recommend that you carry field guides for mammals, birds, butterflies, dragonflies, and wildflowers in your vehicle at all times. Which field guide you toss in a daypack or backpack is up to you. But the best strategy is to leave the field guides behind or carry one or two with you. Take notes and draw sketches, however crude, of wildlife you see while hiking, and compare your notes and drawings to illustrations in the field guides.

It is also a good idea to study field guides before you go on a hike in order to familiarize yourself with the plants and animals you encounter.

Magnifying Glass

Many things in the desert are small and need a closer look. We carry a small magnifying glass in our backpack and a ten-power geologist's loupe to examine such things as bugs, flower blossoms, and minerals laced in rocks. We also find that a magnifying glass and geologist's loupe are helpful in finding a tiny splinter or cactus thorn embedded in our hands or legs.

Please warn children NEVER to start a fire with a magnifying glass by concentrating sunlight on dry vegetation.

Journal

We both carry a journal when we visit the park. Often the journals are no more than a spiral-bound notebook, but occasionally the journals are fine leather-bound notebooks given us by friends. The journals get filled with thoughts, observations, and sketches.

Give a journal to each member of your party. Encourage daily journal entries and allow quiet time for writing. The memories written in journals will provide a priceless record of your experiences in the park.

Sketch Pad

We often see people in the park sitting quietly under the shade of a tree drawing or painting a scene on a sketch pad. The beauty of Big Bend compels artists to create. Should you have an artistic flair or are trying to develop an artistic side, carry a sketch pad along with pencils, crayons, ink, or pastels.

Park Rules

Observe the posted rules around the park. The rules exist for your health and safety as well as for the preservation of the park. Some of the most common rules are also common sense.

■ When you go hiking, tell someone where you are going and when you will be back.

■ When you park your vehicle at a trailhead, leave a note on the dashboard telling people where you are and when you will be back.

■ Keep small children in sight at all times.

■ Stay on the trails to prevent land erosion and damage to flora.

■ Do not collect wildlife, plants, or artifacts. Leave them for future generations.

■ Do not illuminate wildlife with flashlights or spotlights.

Bears and Mountain Lions

Bears and mountain lions are the largest mammals in Big Bend National Park. Respect them—don't fear them—respect them. Respect leads to correct behaviors toward the big creatures.

Read the signs posted throughout the park regarding bears and lions, and heed the advice and warnings. Always keep children close at hand on hikes or in campgrounds. Never let children stroll anywhere in the park unattended. If you do encounter a bear or lion, keep your distance. In most cases, if you leave the bear or lion alone, it will leave you alone. But should the animal be too close for comfort, try to scare it away by bunching up with friends or family members and waving your arms in the air while yelling at the top of your lungs. But never try to provoke a lion whether near or far by trying to charge at it. Never approach a bear, and never try to offer it food.

Bears in particular are attracted to the odoriferous foods and even toiletries of people. So, keep all food and toiletries locked away in the bear-proof boxes near every campsite. On day hikes, store food you're not going to carry with you in the bear-proof boxes located at most parking areas near trailheads.

Your chances of seeing either one of these magnificent beasts are slim. That said, you are more likely to encounter a black bear than a mountain lion. For instance, we have spent over thirty years of countless hours hiking trails in the park, and we can count on the fingers of one hand the number of times we've seen a black bear. We've seen a mountain lion only twice, and those sightings were separated by twenty years.

The Ranger Station in the Chisos Basin keeps a log of all bear and mountain lion sightings. Check out the log and have a talk with the ranger if you're concerned about a particular area. Rangers are the best source of information, and they have both your safety and the well-being of the animals in mind.

If you find yourself on a trail after a rainstorm, watch for bear or mountain lion tracks in the soft mud. (Field guides to animal tracks are available at the Ranger Stations.) Finding fresh bear or lion tracks can be just as exciting as seeing the beast itself. A lot safer, too.

Adventures in Big Bend

I N this book, we offer you a guide to exploring the park no matter how much time you have to spend. We have learned from our own experiences and from those of others that the park can seem overwhelming. It is a vast place. What do you do if you can only spend a half day in the park? A full day? Two days? A week? To answer those questions, we've designed memorable adventures that will meet almost any time frame. We've detailed adventures for our friends who are physically fit as well as for those with limited physical mobility. What's important is that you do something in the park that lets you leave with an unforgettable experience—and the park holds so many experiences, no matter the length of your stay or limitations of your abilities.

We also know how to enjoy the park with children, having taken our own children and grandchildren there many times. Natural wonders in the park offer children a far more spellbinding playground than artifices of human construction, and once children catch on to it, their joy is unstoppable.

All we ask is that you explore what interests you. Explore what captures your imagination. Walk, hike, drive. Look, smell, feel. Take pictures. Draw pictures. Hum melodies. Whatever you do, have a good old-fashioned adventure because adventures in Big Bend are without equal.

Sunrise on Lost Mine Trail

Key to Icons

 Spring

 Summer

 Fall

 Winter

 Daytime

 Nighttime

 Car

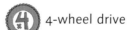 4-wheel drive

 On foot

 Family

 Adults

 Limited mobility

 Physically fit

Black swallowtail

Two-Hour Adventures

Window View

Learn and Snack at Panther Junction

Starting Point: Panther Junction Ranger Station
Ending Point: Service station nearby
Time to Complete Adventure: 1–2 hours
Distance on Foot: About 0.1 mile
Distance in Vehicle: Less than 0.25 mile
Degree of Difficulty: Easy
Preferred Time of Year: Any season
Preferred Start Time: Anytime during the day
Age Group: All ages
Equipment Needed: 8 ounces of water per hour per person,
  hat, and sunglasses

STOP at the Panther Junction Ranger Station to get an overview of Big Bend National Park. A large-scale relief model of the park in the lobby shows major locations, roadways, campgrounds, and mountain ranges. In addition, the Ranger Station offers an excellent bookstore, historical displays, and knowledgeable staff. Ask one of the staff for the logbooks containing recent sightings of unusual birds, butterflies, and mammals.

Don't Miss: The Panther Path self-guided nature trail is an excellent way to learn about the plants that make up the Chihuahuan Desert. The Park Service provides an informative pamphlet for a small fee that gives a brief description of each plant, including common and scientific names.

Enhance Your Adventure: Common desert birds usually flutter around the Ranger Station. Look for cactus wren, canyon towhee, and house finch on any of the bushes along the nature trail or in the parking lot.

Canyon towhee

After visiting the Ranger Station, drive to the nearby service station for a snack. Groceries and souvenirs are available as well as gasoline.

Follow-up to This Adventure: Visits to the Ranger Station at Persimmon Gap, Rio Grande Village, or the Basin

Walk the Trail from the Chisos Mountains Lodge to the Chisos Basin Campground

Starting Point: Chisos Basin Trailhead
Ending Point: Chisos Basin Campground near Amphitheater
Time to Complete Adventure: Less than 2 hours
Distance on Foot: Less than 1 mile
Distance in Vehicle: No vehicle access
Degree of Difficulty: Easy to moderate
Preferred Time of Year: Any season
Preferred Start Time: Anytime during the day
Age Group: All ages; an enjoyable trail for small children or family groups
Equipment Needed: 8–16 ounces of water per person and well-fitting shoes

THE hike takes you along a rocky but well-maintained trail. The trail begins near the Basin store and heads down a steep hillside. Splendid views of the campground, the Window View, and Casa Grande are within sight all along the way. A few steep grades may challenge you, but none is terribly difficult, even if you're the tenderest of tenderfoots. If you're accustomed to hilly walks, the trail will be an invigorating stroll. If you're accustomed to flatland walks, the trail will accelerate your heartbeat. No matter your physical fitness, you'll find plenty of places to stand and rest. No need to rush. Stop and enjoy the views. If you have children, let them romp gleefully up the trail but, as always, never out of sight.

Don't Miss: Look for Carmen white-tailed deer grazing the grassy slopes in the early mornings or late afternoons. Watch for rock squirrels hunched on boulders and sporting dark heads and bushy tails. Also,

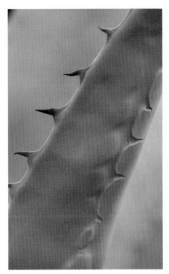

◄ Rock squirrel
▲ Havard agave

look for acorn woodpeckers with their bright red-and-white harlequin faces peering around the trunks of dead trees.

Enhance Your Adventure: Carry a magnifying glass for close-up views of flowers and cacti blooms. Carry binoculars to look at birds and other wildlife. Notice how thorns grow on the Havard agaves, leaving imprints on the adjacent leaves. Havard agaves (also called century plants) in the Big Bend Basin take about 20–30 years to bloom by erecting a tall stalk rimmed by branches holding bright yellow flowers resembling candles in a candelabra. Next, look for rubbish piles at the base of prickly-pear cacti, piles that are probably wood rat nests. Wood rats, sometimes called pack-rats, use natural materials like leaves and sotol threads to construct their nests but also use human litter like string, shoelaces, and pieces of foil.

Follow-up to This Adventure: Chisos Basin Loop Trail

Walk the Chisos Basin Loop Trail

Starting and Ending Point: Chisos Basin Trailhead
Time to Complete Adventure: 1–2 hours
Distance on Foot: 1.6 miles
Distance in Vehicle: None
Degree of Difficulty: Easy to moderate. Steep sections of the trail are edged in cedar logs or rocks to ease your walk up or down. The trail also widens and flares out at certain bends so that you may stop, stand, and take in the beautiful vistas.
Preferred Time of Year: Any season
Preferred Start Time: Anytime during the day, but early morning or late afternoon is best
Age Group: 5 years to adult
Equipment Needed: 8 ounces of water per hour per person, a light snack, closed-toed hiking boots, hat, sunscreen, and sunglasses

THE Chisos Basin Loop is a good way to experience the flora and fauna of the high Chisos. If you're unable to hike up the mountains, take this trail as an efficient way to experience the beauty of the Chisos Mountains. Parents with small children will enjoy this trail because it offers an abundance of natural treasures like deer, birds, and flowering plants.

Even though encounters with mammals are rare during the day, you'll see plenty of scat, or animal poop, left behind by such critters as deer, fox, and rabbits that traversed the trail during the night. Some of the scat will be full of hair, which indicates that the animal excreting it was a carnivore, such as a fox, that ate a mammal, perhaps a rat. Scat full of seeds indicates that it came from a fruit-eating animal, such as a javelina.

Don't Miss: Examine the various species of trees that cover the surface of the mountain. Try to find the alligator juniper, weeping juniper, pon-

Casa Grande

derosa pine, gray oak, and Emory oak. Look for lechuguilla, sotol, Havard agave, and bear grass. Notice the many different varieties of grass that grow along the trail. Don't forget to look at wildflowers, butterflies, and birds.

Enhance Your Adventure: Carry binoculars to watch birds, butterflies, and other creatures. Bring your camera or sketch pad to record sights you see. Walking sticks are a great tool to steady your feet on the loose rocks.

Follow-up to This Adventure: Pinnacles Trail, Laguna Meadow Trail, Southwest Rim Trail, or Lost Mine Trail

Enjoy a Journey
on Dagger Yucca Drive

Starting and Ending Point: Persimmon Gap Ranger Station or
Panther Junction Station
Time to Complete Adventure: 2 hours
Distance on Foot: Minimal
Distance in Vehicle: 26 miles
Degree of Difficulty: Easy
Preferred Time of Year: Spring
Preferred Start Time: Anytime during the day, but morning is best
Age Group: All ages
Equipment Needed: 8 ounces of water per person per hour and
at least half a tank of gas

DAGGER yuccas are the largest of the four yuccas in Big Bend and can be found in the eastern part of the park. These giants of the desert can reach heights of 20 feet. They bloom only once a year in the spring, hoisting up a single flower stalk weighing up to 70 pounds. A drive along Highway 385 in the spring provides delightful views of these beautiful plants as well as other blooming yuccas and wildflowers.

Don't Miss: Park your car at any of the numerous pull-offs along the highway. Walk to one of the yuccas to get a close look at the flower stalk. Notice that the stalk contains hundreds of blooms. Watch the bees, hummingbirds, and other creatures of the desert visiting the blooms.

Enhance Your Adventure: Drive the Dagger Flats Auto Trail to Dagger Flats. The 14-mile round-trip along an improved dirt road will give you a close encounter with the big yuccas that stand tall, sturdy, and elegant

Dagger
yucca

as if defying the dearth of water in the desert. Pick up a guide to Dagger Flats, available at the Ranger Stations for a small fee.

Follow-up to This Adventure: A drive to see wildflowers along any of the paved roads in the park

Half-Day
Adventures

Window
Trail

Drive and Hike Rio Grande Village and Boquillas Canyon

Starting Point: Rio Grande Village
Ending Point: Boquillas Canyon parking area
Time to Complete Adventure: 2–4 hours
Distance on Foot: 1.4 miles at Boquillas
Distance in Vehicle: 5 miles from Rio Grande Village
Degree of Difficulty: Medium
Preferred Time of Year: Any season
Preferred Start Time: In summer, start out early in the morning because humidity and heat at midday can make for a vicious trek. In winter, the hike is reasonably comfortable almost any time of the day.
Age Group: 5 years to adult
Equipment Needed: 8 ounces of water per hour per person

RIO Grande Village includes a store with showers, a laundry, and restrooms. The village has ample places for tent and RV camping, although the camping areas may be crowded from October through April. The store stocks food and miscellaneous supplies for both campers and day visitors. The Ranger Station is open from November to April and contains exhibits and a bookstore. Rio Grande Village is also a good starting point for an adventure to Boquillas Canyon.

Boquillas Canyon is a narrow canyon that squeezes and whips the Rio Grande nearly 180 degrees from west to north. The hike into the canyon begins in the parking lot at the end of the spur road. The trail leads over a small hill and then turns to face the Rio Grande and Mexico. At the hill, notice the mortars, or metates, in the limestone rock slab. The holes were made by Native Americans as they ground mesquite seeds into a flourlike substance. Take a moment to touch the holes and gaze out over the vista. Imagine what it was like in ancient times to prepare an evening meal from the vantage point of this hill overlooking the

Bouquillas
Canyon

Rio Grande and Boquillas Canyon. After you hike up the hillside, past the mortars, past the hill, through the river cane, and across the loose sand, you arrive at Boquillas Canyon. Look up at the canyon wall on the right side and notice a prominent diagonal line, a geologic fault, which illustrates how one side of the limestone wall is moving against the other side.

Don't Miss: Climb the sand dunes at Boquillas Canyon up to the shallow cave, assuming your legs are willing to trudge through the deep sand.

Enhance Your Adventure: When the river is low, examine the smooth, water-polished rocks along the banks.

Follow-up to This Adventure: A snack and cold drink at the Rio Grande Village store

Drive and Learn about Geology on Ross Maxwell Scenic Drive

Starting Point: The intersection of Park Road 118 and Ross Maxwell Scenic Drive
Ending Point: La Harmonia store at Castolon
Time to Complete Adventure: 2–4 hours
Distance on Foot: Minimal
Distance in Vehicle: 22 miles
Degree of Difficulty: Easy
Preferred Time of Year: Any season
Preferred Start Time: Anytime during the day, but early morning or midafternoon is best
Age Group: 5 years to adult
Equipment Needed: 8 ounces of water per hour per person. Even though this is a car trip, your body will lose moisture in the desert.

THE drive is named for Ross Maxwell, who became superintendent of Big Bend National Park on July 16, 1944, twenty-three days after the National Park Service received title to the land. Roads in the park were relatively primitive at first, but Ross Maxwell began an extensive road-building and road-improvement campaign that lasted until 1965. In 1984, the road to Castolon was officially designated the Ross Maxwell Scenic Drive.

The drive offers a survey of Big Bend geology. Pull-offs scattered along the length of the road have markers with descriptions and explanations of the geologic features. The first marker describes Ward Mountain rising up across the desert floor. Stop and read the sign to learn that Ward Mountain is a large intrusion of igneous rock that forms the western side of the Chisos Mountains.

Geologic marvels such as dikes, strata, lava-topped plateaus, and canyons of pyroclastic debris and ash await you along the drive. Stop at

Mule Ears Peaks

every pull-off and read the signs. Scan the geologic features with your binoculars, take pictures, and touch the nearby rocks.

Don't Miss: Look at Mule Ears Peaks, which were used by early travelers as a landmark. Observe Goat Mountain, where an ancient streambed exposed on the mountainside once cut a canyon 900 feet deep.

Enhance Your Adventure: Buy any of the books for sale in the park or those recommended at the end of this book on the geology of the park. Big Bend National Park shows off spectacular geologic features. Once you understand and appreciate the forces that created the terrain, your appreciation of the park will soar.

Follow-up to This Adventure: Enjoy a picnic at La Harmonia store at Castolon or Cottonwood Campground. Sunset on Cerro Castellan is a sight you won't soon forget.

Hike and Picnic on the Window Trail

Starting and Ending Point: Chisos Basin Trailhead or Chisos Basin Campground
Time to Complete Adventure: 3–4 hours
Distance on Foot: 5.6 miles from the Chisos Basin or 4.4 miles from the campground
Distance in Vehicle: None
Degree of Difficulty: Easy going down; a killer coming up
Preferred Time of Year: Any season
Preferred Start Time: Early morning in warm months; midmorning in the cool months
Age Group: 5 years to adult
Equipment Needed: 32–64 ounces of water per person, hiking boots or sturdy shoes, hat, sunscreen, and sunglasses

THE Window Trail offers one of the most beautiful treks in the park. It descends from the cool mountains across flat, open scrubland and arrives at a shady creek bed with rugged cliffs towering overhead. The trail ends at a slick pour-off, forming the base of the V in the Window that was formed by creek water slicing through the canyon over eons. The view is incredible. And nothing beats a picnic lunch at the pour-off.

The agony comes on the return trip. Every step back is at an incline. The 2-mile hike down is relatively easy, but the return hike up a 500- to 980-foot rise in elevation challenges leg muscles and lung capacity. Time your hike so that you're not ascending out of the canyon in the heat of the day with the sun beating down on you.

We've often seen people stand at the Basin Trailhead reading about the Window Trail, and saying, "Oh, look, it's only two miles. Let's go!" And off they go, sometimes with children in tow, often having flip-flops for footwear, and carrying no water and wearing no hats. For them, an otherwise

Sleepy Orange

joyful hike becomes a grueling—if not a somewhat dangerous—feat.
Never hike the trails without sturdy footwear, ample water, and a hat.

Don't Miss: Look for animal tracks on the trail, rabbits in the brush,
and loads of butterflies and birds in summertime. If you're a birder,
butterfly watcher, or dragonfly enthusiast, you should put this hike at
the top of your list.

Enhance Your Adventure: Take a picnic lunch and eat at the pour-off at
the end of the trail. Don't hurry. You're not on a race to a finish line.
Take time to explore every scene, every critter, and every plant that
catches your fancy.

Follow-up to This Adventure: Lunch or dinner in the Chisos Mountains Lodge

A Full-Day Adventure

Teenage bird-watcher on the South Rim

Hike to the Southwest Rim

Starting and Ending Point: Chisos Basin Trailhead
Time to Complete Adventure: 6–8 hours
Distance on Foot: 12–13 miles
Distance in Vehicle: None
Degree of Difficulty: Difficult to extremely difficult
Preferred Time of Year: Spring through fall
Preferred Start Time: Early in the morning to beat the heat and maximize the time at high elevations
Age Group: 10 years to adult
Equipment Needed: 64 ounces of water per person, snacks or lunch, sturdy hiking boots, hat, sunscreen, sunglasses, and trail map. A jacket and rain gear are always suggested; a light jacket is recommended even in the summer because a sudden rainstorm can dramatically lower mountain temperatures.

THE Southwest Rim rests 7,500 feet above sea level but only 2,500 feet above the desert floor. It offers a jaw-dropping view of the surrounding desert and mountains. On a clear day, mountains 100 miles to the south in Mexico are visible. The hike requires stamina, even for people in good physical condition, but you'll have less strain on your muscles and tendons, besides having more fun, by taking the hike at a leisurely pace. Start at daybreak, and make the hike an all-day affair.

The hike begins at the Chisos Basin Trailhead. You may choose one of two routes to ascend the high peaks of the Chisos Mountains. First is the Laguna Meadow Trail, which makes a gradual ascent covering about 5.8 miles via switchbacks through open terrain. (Switchbacks are trails that zigzag up mountainsides and ease the strain of the steep grades.) The second route is the Pinnacles Trail, which ascends steeply for about 3.5 miles and then through Boot Canyon for about 2.8 miles to the Southwest Rim, with most of the journey through shaded forests. Whatever your route, the last mile to the Southwest Rim is relatively easy. We

Mexican jay

suggest you hike up the mountain via one route and down the other route to enjoy the full splendor of the mountain scenery.

Hiking to the Southwest Rim is a badge of honor. "Did you go to the Southwest Rim?" is a common question people will ask about your trip to the park.

Don't Miss: Enjoy Boot Canyon, a remote, lush, montane forest filled with birds, butterflies, mammals, and trees such as Arizona cypress, ponderosa pine, and Douglas fir. Your best chance of encountering a black bear will be in this canyon. Birders hike to Boot Canyon in the spring and summer to see the Colima warbler, which nests in the United States only in this canyon and in the high mountains of Fort Davis. If you unpack a lunch at the picnic table at Boot Springs by the Ranger cabin, you may find yourself fending off Mexican jays that want a bite of your food. (Remember, it's illegal to feed animals in the park.)

Enhance Your Adventure: Carry binoculars to watch birds and butterflies along the way. Stop to enjoy the solitude of Boot Canyon. You may make this hike only once in your lifetime. Take time to relish the experience.

Follow-up to This Adventure: Dinner and dessert at Chisos Mountains Lodge

Adventures with Families and Small Children

Couch's spadefoot toad

Take a Nighttime Drive to Look for Mammals and Reptiles

Starting and Ending Point: Any road
Time to Complete Adventure: 1–2 hours
Distance on Foot: Minimal
Distance in Vehicle: Varies depending on length of adventure
Degree of Difficulty: Easy
Preferred Time of Year: Spring, summer, and fall
Preferred Start Time: At sunset or 2 hours before dawn
Age Group: 5 years to adult
Equipment Needed: 8 ounces of water per hour per person, flashlight, and safety equipment for nighttime travel

BECAUSE desert mammals and reptiles come out in the cool of the evening, your best opportunity to see a coyote, fox, jackrabbit, or snake is within an hour or two of dusk or dawn. Start your drive near your campground or hotel. Drive slowly along the road, and watch for eye-shine from mammals, birds, and frogs. Keep your speed in the range of 10–15 miles per hour so you can stop before you hit a critter.

Snakes slink out on warm road surfaces at dusk. Stop for every stick in the road or tan-colored crack. Assume that most objects are snakes, and stop before running over any snakelike object. (Remember, it's illegal to kill or capture any critter in the park, even snakes. Running over a snake is against the law, a federal law at that.)

Don't Miss: During the spring and summer, whip-poor-wills, common poorwills, and nighthawks rest on the road. They fly up to catch insects attracted to oncoming vehicle headlights. Drive slowly to avoid hitting the birds as they zip through your vehicle's headlight beams.

▲ Big Bend at night

◀ Curve-billed thrasher

Enhance Your Adventure: Carry a camera with a flash to photograph nocturnal creatures. Remember, handling wildlife is against park rules as well as being potentially dangerous.

Follow-up to This Adventure: A star-watching party or sunrise-watching party

Explore the Sam Nail Ranch Homestead

Starting and Ending Point: Parking area at Sam Nail Ranch
Time to Complete Adventure: 2–3 hours
Distance on Foot: Less than 1 mile
Distance in Vehicle: None
Degree of Difficulty: Easy
Preferred Time of Year: Any season
Preferred Start Time: Anytime during the day, but early morning is best
Age Group: 5 years to adult
Equipment Needed: 8 ounces of water per hour per person

SAM Nail started working on his homestead in 1916 with his brother, Jim. They dug a well and constructed a one-story adobe house. Sam married Nena Burnam, from nearby Government Spring, and they stayed on the property until 1944. Little remains today of the adobe house with the concrete floor and sheet-metal roof. No longer can you see the pens where Sam kept milk cows or the chicken coop where he raised chickens and collected their eggs, but you will see remnant fruit trees like walnut, pecan, and fig that he planted.

We enjoy going to Sam Nail Ranch at dawn to listen to the chorus of birds. We have found birdsong to be most intense during the mating season, when male birds sing on the tops of conspicuous perches to claim breeding territories and attract females. The Park Service has created a series of earthen trails through the site. Walk each trail, and listen to the birds singing in the desert oasis.

Don't Miss: In spring and summer, painted buntings, varied buntings, curve-billed thrashers, and a variety of other birds sing from the top of yucca, prickly-pear cactus, and mesquite.

Sunrise in the desert

Enhance Your Adventure: Visit the displays at Panther Junction Ranger Station. Or, for an exhibit of early life in the Big Bend region, go to the Castolon visitor center.

Follow-up to This Adventure: A visit to the Blue Creek Ranch 4 miles south along Ross Maxwell Scenic Drive

Journey through Time at
Hot Springs Historic Area

Starting and Ending Point: Hot Springs parking area
Time to Complete Adventure: 1–2 hours
Distance on Foot: 2 miles round-trip
Distance in Vehicle: Less than 5 miles from Rio Grande Village
    or 20 miles from Panther Junction Ranger Station
Degree of Difficulty: Easy
Preferred Time of Year: Any season
Preferred Start Time: Anytime during the day. However, be aware
    that it can be brutally hot at midday in summer.
Age Group: All ages
Equipment Needed: 8 ounces of water per hour per person, hat,
    sunscreen, and sunglasses

YOU might not detect it at first, but Hot Springs was a thriving
community for much of the first quarter of the twentieth century.
The first building you see on the left was a store and post office where
mail came every Monday. On "mail day," people throughout the Big
Bend region on both sides of the border came to buy supplies, sell wares
and agricultural goods, and meet neighbors. The building next to the
post office was a motel that housed visitors who came to enjoy the hot
spring water bubbling inside stone-lined tubs by the river. People visited
the spring for what they believed were curative powers of its mineral-
laden water. When the river is high, the remnant stone tubs may not be
visible.

Don't Miss: Observe the murals painted on the walls of the store and
hotel rooms. Etta Koch, a resident of the community in the 1940s, painted the murals in the store. Another resident, Maisie Lee, painted the
murals in the hotel rooms. But long before the paintings of Koch and

Hot Springs complex

Lee, prehistoric people painted pictographs on the limestone walls of the canyon just past the hotel rooms.

Look for the intricate mud nests of cliff swallows high on the canyon walls during spring and summer.

Enhance Your Adventure: The self-guided pamphlet available at the Ranger Stations is filled with historical information about Hot Springs. Also, Etta Koch's book, *Lizards on the Mantle, Burros at the Door,* will give you an unparalleled appreciation of the once-thriving community. Koch lived in the Longfellow House, the stone building on the hill adjacent to the parking area. Walk up to the house to see another mural she painted.

Follow-up to This Adventure: A visit to the Panther Junction Ranger Station to see the exhibit on prehistoric animals that lived in the Big Bend region

Do an Outing with a Topographic Map and Compass

Starting and Ending Point: Anywhere on a map
Time to Complete Adventure: As much time as needed
Distance on Foot: Depends on the terrain and people involved
Distance in Vehicle: None
Degree of Difficulty: Depends on the terrain and people involved
Preferred Time of Year: Any season
Preferred Start Time: Anytime during the day, but early morning or late afternoon is best
Age Group: 5 years to adult
Equipment Needed: 8 ounces of water per hour per person, compass, and topographic map of the study area

A TOPOGRAPHIC map shows a three-dimensional surface on a flat piece of paper. Steep slopes are indicated by contour lines that are close together on the map. Level terrain is shown by contour lines that are wider apart. Hiking trails, roads, and water features are also shown on a topographic map.

Locate by line of sight two hills or mountains indicated on the map. Figure out which feature is taller and which feature has the steeper side. Place a compass on a flat surface and turn it until the red needle points at the letter *N* for the direction north. All other directions can now be determined.

If hiking with children, let them estimate the ascent or descent of a trail by reading the topographic map. Let them take compass readings to determine their location on the trail. Most school-age children take quickly to the map and compass.

Nowadays, GPS handheld units are the rage; some are even integrat-

Casa Grande at sunset

ed into cell phones. If you own a "stand-alone" GPS unit—cell phones don't normally work in the park—use it to navigate the trails. But play with a topographic map and compass, neither of which needs batteries.

Don't Miss: Learn the skill of orienteering with a compass. It could save your life someday.

Enhance Your Adventure: Children 5 or 6 years old might need a simple map. Get trail maps from the Ranger Stations, or use the map of the campground or Chisos Mountains Lodge area. Let children hold a compass and plot progress on the map.

Follow-up to This Adventure: A visit to Panther Junction Ranger Station to see the relief map in the lobby and examine its compass points

Walk the Window View Trail

Starting and Ending Point: Chisos Basin store parking lot
Time to Complete Adventure: Less than 1 hour
Distance on Foot: 0.3 mile
Distance in Vehicle: None
Degree of Difficulty: Easy
Preferred Time of Year: Any season
Preferred Start Time: Anytime during the day
Age Group: Toddler–10 years old (accompanied by an adult)
Equipment Needed: 8 ounces of water per hour per person, hat, and sunglasses

THE Window View Trail offers a comfortable path on a paved surface with benches at two overlook locations. The trail loops around an open, grassy area where Carmen white-tailed deer frequently graze. Lizards often bask in the sunshine on top of rocks. A trail guide is available at the trailhead for a small fee.

Don't Miss: Look for Carmen white-tailed deer and javelina walking through the grasslands in the morning and late evening. Watch birds like rufous-crowned sparrows and lesser goldfinches feeding on the tall grass heads. Remind children to use a low, quiet voice when on the trail. We call this the "Indian voice." Wildlife and birds are scared off by loud noises.

Enhance Your Adventure: Give the trail map to school-age children. Let them find the brown numbered markers and read about each spot, study plant fibers or bugs with a magnifying glass, and look at spider webs wedged between prickly-pear cactus pads.

Follow-up to This Adventure: Panther Path at Panther Junction and Rio Grande Village Nature Trail

◄ Carmen white-tailed deer
▼ Pipevine swallowtail
▼▼ Monarch butterfly

Enjoy a Scavenger Hunt

Starting and Ending Point: Anywhere in the park
Time to Complete Adventure: Child's attention span
Distance on Foot: Up to the child
Distance in Vehicle: None, except to travel to a specific location
Degree of Difficulty: Easy
Preferred Time of Year: Any season
Preferred Start Time: Anytime during the day
Age Group: 4–12 years (accompanied by adult)
Equipment Needed: 8 ounces of water per hour per person and hat

CHILDREN love to walk and explore in Big Bend. One way to encourage exploration is to go on a scavenger hunt. Work with the child's cognitive level and interests to find the subjects of your scavenger hunt. One child might want to look for animals, so the scavenger hunt would involve looking for deer, javelina, and rock squirrels around the lodge or campground. Another child might want to look for birds, butterflies, or blooming cacti found in a field guide. Maybe a child wants to look at rocks of various shapes and sizes. The subject of the scavenger hunt is not important. What's important is getting out, walking, and letting a child satisfy an innate curiosity.

A field guide with clear photos or drawings is a good way to show a child what to hunt for. Or simply let the child find plants and animals depicted on postcards of Big Bend National Park. However, remind children that they cannot collect objects. Federal law strictly prohibits the collection of plants, animals, rocks, or artifacts in national parks.

Don't Miss: Remember that each child is different. The child with an avid interest in birds and butterflies might stay engaged in the scavenger hunt for hours. Another child might stay with the hunt for only an hour at a time. Don't worry. Whatever captures the imagination of your child

◄ Desert lubber grasshopper

▲ Young bird-watcher field guide

for whatever length of time is fine. The idea is to allow your child the joy of exploration.

Enhance Your Adventure: Visit any Ranger Station to see the exhibits. The taxidermy animals, the displays of plants, or exhibits of historical items might spark your child's interest.

Follow-up to This Adventure: A stop at a nearby concession area for a cold drink and snack

Adventures for the Physically Fit

Hiker on
a Big Bend
trail

Hike to Boot Canyon

Starting and Ending Point: Chisos Basin Trailhead
Time to Complete Adventure: 3–6 hours
Distance on Foot: 9 miles round-trip
Distance in Vehicle: None
Degree of Difficulty: Strenuous
Preferred Time of Year: Any season, but spring, summer, and fall are best
Preferred Start Time: Early morning to give enough time to explore and enjoy
Age Group: 5 years to adult
Equipment Needed: 48 ounces of water per person, lunch and snacks, sturdy hiking boots, hat, sunscreen, sunglasses, lip balm, and first-aid kit with blister protection

A S one of the most visited high-country locations in the Chisos Mountains, Boot Canyon derives its name from a rock spire in the canyon that looks like an upside-down cowboy boot. Experienced Big Bend hikers simply call the canyon "The Boot." The canyon is fed by spring water from Boot Springs.

Scores of birders make the half-day journey to Boot Canyon every spring and summer to see the Colima warbler. The drab, brownish gray bird nests in the shady, moist, oak-lined canyon. Boot Canyon and other canyons in the Chisos Mountains were once the only place people could see the Colima warbler in the United States, but the bird has recently been discovered at Mount Livermore in the Davis Mountains 130 miles to the north.

Wildlife abounds in Boot Canyon. Mexican jays and black-crested titmice are common at the picnic tables by the Park Service cabin near where the Pinnacles Trail and Boot Springs Trail meet. Butterflies like California sister, Mead's wood-nymph, and southern dogface sip nectar on abundant wildflowers during the warm months. Blue-throated

Boot formation

hummingbirds nest in the trees along the creek formed by Boot Springs. Dragonflies, lizards, frogs, and occasionally a bear may be found near the deeper pools of water.

Don't Miss: Look for the Colima warbler. Enjoy the solitude. Boot Canyon is a place far above—literally, far above—the din of urban life.

Enhance Your Adventure: Carry field guides for birds, butterflies, and wildflowers. Carry a camera or sketch pad to record your sightings. Make detailed written notes of critters and wildflowers you see so you can study them later.

Follow-up to This Adventure: Dinner in the Chisos Mountains Lodge and a stroll to the Window View for a stunning sunset scene

Hike to Emory Peak

Starting and Ending Point: Chisos Basin Trailhead
Time to Complete Adventure: Half day to a full day
Distance on Foot: 9 miles round-trip
Distance in Vehicle: None
Degree of Difficulty: Strenuous
Preferred Time of Year: When the weather is warm. Temperatures may drop dramatically in any season, even in midsummer, as you ascend the mountain.
Preferred Start Time: Early morning to give enough time to explore and enjoy
Age Group: 10 years to adult
Equipment Needed: 64 ounces of water per person, lunch and snacks, sturdy hiking boots, hat, sunscreen, sunglasses, lip balm, and first-aid kit with blister protection

EMORY PEAK is the highest point in Big Bend National Park and the tenth-highest point in Texas. Rising 7,825 feet above sea level, the peak ascends 2,425 feet above the mile-high Chisos Basin.

We recommend hiking the Pinnacles Trail from the Chisos Basin Trailhead up the mountain toward Emory Peak. Even though the Pinnacles Trail is a knee-crunching climb, it saves time and energy in the long run. Besides, it winds through terrain covered in such trees as oaks, juniper, maple, and madrone. At the end of Pinnacles Trail is Pinnacles Pass, where you can rest and visit the composting toilet before heading up the trail to Mount Emory's summit.

Emory Peak Trail covers merely a mile, but the last hundred feet to the top taxes legs, tendons, and joints. Near the end, you'll scramble over boulders and pull yourself up a sheer rock face to reach the pinnacle that holds the park's radio antenna and miscellaneous instruments. But the view from the top is worth every aching knee and thigh.

Pinnacles Trail

Don't Miss: Savor the panoramic view from Emory Peak. You'll look down on the Basin, Casa Grande, the Southwest Rim, and a vast stretch of the Chihuahuan Desert.

Enhance Your Adventure: Watch white-throated swifts (common except in winter months) whiz and whirl past your head. You can hear the wind rushing over their wings as they fly through the air at blazing speeds.

Follow-up to This Adventure: A hike into Boot Springs to relax before descending to the Basin

Hike to Dog Canyon or Devil's Den

Starting and Ending Point: Parking area on Highway 385 approximately 3.5 miles from Persimmon Gap Visitor Center at Nine Point Draw
Time to Complete Adventure: Half day to a full day
Distance on Foot: 5 miles to Dog Canyon and 5.6 miles to Devil's Den, or 10–11.2 miles round-trip
Distance in Vehicle: None
Degree of Difficulty: Moderately difficult to difficult
Preferred Time of Year: October through April. The hike can be mercilessly hot from May to September. If you're hiking during these months, it is best to start at dawn so you can return before the intense heat of midday.
Preferred Start Time: Early morning. Even in winter months, the hike can be painfully hot at midday.
Age Group: Teenagers to adult (best for experienced hikers)
Equipment Needed: 64 ounces of water per person, lunch and snacks, hat, topographic map, park-issued trail map, compass, appropriate clothing for the weather, flashlight, first-aid kit with blister protection, and a rope

THE trails to Dog Canyon and Devil's Den are primitive and poorly marked. Therefore, we recommend you use a topographic map of the area on this hike.

Dog Canyon is visible from the first trail marker and remains visible during the entire hike. It looks like a craggy slot through the Santiago Mountains. Hike the cairn-marked trail for 1.5 miles until you reach a dry creek bed called an arroyo. Follow the arroyo directly to the left 0.25 mile into Dog Canyon.

If you follow the arroyo to the right, you'll intersect a second arroyo about a half mile away. Follow the second arroyo to the left 0.8 mile to reach Devil's Den, a dramatic 0.6-mile-long and 80- to 90-foot-deep gash in the side of the mountain south of Dog Canyon. The gash looks

Southern dogface

as though a colossal Jack-the-Ripper slashed his knife across the mountain slope. You may hike down into the abrupt canyon, but be cautious of slippery rocks and water-laden potholes.

Don't Miss: Enjoy a spectacular view from Devil's Den of a valley in the Dead Horse Mountains. Look for glistening quartz outcrops in the arroyos.

Enhance Your Adventure: Carry a topographic map and necessary supplies to ensure you have a safe adventure.

Follow-up to This Adventure: Nice hot bath

Hike to the Chimneys

Starting and Ending Point: Ross Maxwell Scenic Drive past Burro Mesa
  Pour-off
Time to Complete Adventure: 3–4 hours
Distance on Foot: 4.8 miles round-trip
Distance in Vehicle: None
Degree of Difficulty: Easy but can be very hot in the summer
Preferred Time of Year: October through March or early in the morning
  during the summer
Preferred Start Time: Anytime during the day, but early morning or late
  afternoon is best
Age Group: 5 years to adult
Equipment Needed: 32 ounces of water or more per person, snack, sturdy
  hiking boots, hat, sunscreen, coat, or rain gear depending on the weather
  and season, and long pants

YOU can spot the Chimneys from the trailhead parking area off
Ross Maxwell Scenic Drive. The rocky outcrops resembling artistic
sculptures are part of a geologic feature called a dike. The trail to the
Chimneys is relatively flat and easy to traverse. Although the distance is
only 2.5 miles, the hike can be deceptively tough because of the rugged
terrain of loose rock and thorny plants like cacti and lechuguilla that
can stab your legs in an instant. Wear long pants on this hike to protect
your legs.

Once you reach the Chimneys, look for Native American petroglyphs
on the side of the southernmost chimney. Crosses, a bisected circle, and
snakelike drawings give you a glimpse into the handicraft of ancient
people. Sadly, some of the carvings have been defaced by bullets. Keep
in mind that prehistoric and historic sites in the park are protected by
federal law. Leave them untouched as a legacy for future generations.

In the days of European exploration of the Big Bend, the Chimneys

◀ Pictograph at the Chimneys

▲ Redeye prickly-pear

provided a landmark for navigation across the desert. Look at marks on the Chimneys from the early explorers.

Don't Miss: Gaze through an opening called the keyhole on the side of the Chimneys. Use it to frame a photograph of the surrounding landscape.

Enhance Your Adventure: Look for blooming cacti if you hike in the spring. Because cacti bloom well after sunrise, look for the blooms on your return hike.

Follow-up to This Adventure: Lunch or snack at La Harmonia store at Castolon

Explore Santa Elena Canyon

Starting and Ending Point: The parking area at the end of Ross Maxwell Scenic Drive
Time to Complete Adventure: 1–2 hours
Distance on Foot: 1.7 miles
Distance in Vehicle: None
Degree of Difficulty: Moderately difficult due to a walk across loose sand and an ascent up stairs along the cliff face
Preferred Time of Year: Any season. Check river conditions first to be sure you can cross Terlingua Creek.
Preferred Start Time: Anytime during the day, but early morning or late afternoon is best
Age Group: 5 years to adult
Equipment Needed: 16–24 ounces of water per person, snacks, sturdy hiking boots, hat, sunscreen, and sunglasses

THE Rio Grande formed Santa Elena Canyon over the eons by eroding away limestone layers of the Sierra Ponce. The canyon begins near Lajitas in the low-lying desert and comes to a dramatic end at the Santa Elena Canyon trailhead where the muddy Rio Grande cuts through 1,500-foot cliffs.

The majority of the canyon is visible only by floating down the river on a raft or in a canoe. Nonetheless, the Santa Elena Canyon Trail gives foot-bound visitors an exhilarating view of a fabulous geologic formation.

The trail begins in the parking area and then descends into the sandy deposits of Terlingua Creek. The loose sand can make for a challenging walk. Terlingua Creek is normally a tranquil, narrow stream that is easy to cross by striding over muddy outcrops and rocks. But during the summer rainy season, the creek can become a raging torrent, impossible to walk across. Even when the flooding creek subsides, it leaves thick mud that might suck in your legs up to the knees. Be careful. Assuming

Santa Elena Canyon

you can cross the creek, the trail continues up a rock outcrop with the aid of concrete steps and a handrail. It then winds along the riverbank through cane and other vegetation to a rock wall at the end.

Don't Miss: Look for the large boulders in the river. Think of the sounds these rocks made when they fell from the surrounding cliffs.

Enhance Your Adventure: Watch for birds. Listen to a canyon wren calling from the cliffs. The call is a descending, liquid *tee-tee-tee* sound that seems like the bird is laughing at you. Watch the skies for coal-black common ravens making a resoundingly deep-throated croaking call that sounds like *crough-crough*. Peregrine falcons nest on the cliff faces, but you'll be lucky to spy one because the birds are inconspicuous against the cliffs.

Follow-up to This Adventure: A snack at La Harmonia store at Castolon

Hit the Hiking Trails

Starting and Ending Point: Trailheads throughout the park
Time to Complete Adventure: 1 hour to all day
Distance on Foot: 1 or more miles
Distance in Vehicle: None
Degree of Difficulty: Easy to strenuous
Preferred Time of Year: Any season
Preferred Start Time: Choose an appropriate time for each trail.
Age Group: 5 years to adult
Equipment Needed: 16–24 ounces or more of water per hour per person, lunch and snacks, sturdy hiking boots, hat, sunscreen, sunglasses, lip balm, and first-aid kit with blister protection

BIG BEND Bend National Park offers a wide variety of hiking trails. Pick up a copy of *Hiker's Guide to Trails of Big Bend National Park*, published by the Big Bend Natural History Association, at any concession area in the park. The guide highlights thirty-six hikes that range from easy to strenuous. Find a hike that fits your fitness and endurance level.

Trails in the park have a best season for hiking. Although every trail can be hiked every month of the year, it's prudent to match the trail to the season. Tackle the desert hikes during the cooler part of the year. Spend the hot summer months hiking the trails through the mountains.

Don't Miss: Pay attention to the daily weather bulletin posted at about eight o'clock each morning. The park is so remote that it is difficult to get an accurate forecast from outside sources. Check the park's weather report before heading out on a long hike.

Enhance Your Adventure: Carry a camera, sketch pad, or journal to record your adventure. Stop along the journey and take in the scenery. Most trails in the park lead to a spectacular site or view. Enjoy the destination.

Claret cup cactus

Follow-up to This Adventure: A hike in a different ecozone the following day

Adventures
at an Easy Pace

Castalon store front porch

View the Sunset at the Window View Trail

Starting and Ending Point: Chisos Basin Trailhead
Time to Complete Adventure: 1 hour
Distance on Foot: 0.3 mile round-trip
Distance in Vehicle: None
Degree of Difficulty: Easy
Preferred Time of Year: Any season
Preferred Start Time: 1 hour before sunset
Age Group: All ages
Equipment Needed: 8 ounces of water per hour per person and a jacket, even in summer

MORE photographs have been taken of the sunset at the Window than of any other scene in Big Bend National Park. From about May to June, the sun sets in the middle of the large V cut between Ward Mountain and Vernon Bailey Peak by water draining from the Basin into the low-lying desert. From about September to April, the sun sets off center from the crux of the V, but the view remains spectacular.

Check sunset times on the daily weather report posted at any Ranger Station, Visitor Center, or concession. The glorious show begins an hour to 45 minutes before sundown, so arrive early to get a good viewing or photography spot. Or just sit down on one of the benches along the Window View Trail and enjoy a scene like no other. As you watch the sunset, notice that the songbirds quiet down as they begin to roost at the setting of the sun. But listen carefully, and you may detect the sounds of owls, whose temporal world is the night.

Don't Miss: Look behind you at Casa Grande, illuminated in golden orange by the last rays of the setting sun.

Sunset through Window View

Enhance Your Adventure: Bring a tripod for your camera to get stunning photographs of the sunset.

Follow-up to This Adventure: Watch the stars pop into view in the evening twilight. During summer, the star Regulus and the crescent moon move in tandem through the twilight sky. Sit on a bench, and gaze at stars shining brilliantly in a sky free from city lights.

Lunch and Learn at Castolon Historical Compound

Starting and Ending Point: La Harmonia store
Time to Complete Adventure: 1–2 hours
Distance on Foot: Minimal to 0.5 mile depending on sites visited
Distance in Vehicle: None
Degree of Difficulty: Easy
Preferred Time of Year: Any season
Preferred Start Time: Anytime during the day. The store closes in the late afternoon, so check closing time before driving to the store.
Age Group: All ages
Equipment Needed: 8 ounces of water per hour per person, walking shoes, and hat

THE Castolon Historical Compound offers a glimpse into the lives of people along the Rio Grande in the late nineteenth and early twentieth centuries. Mexican families were the first settlers to establish productive, long-standing farms in the area. American farmers, ranchers, miners, and merchants followed after Texas became part of the United States.

The compound consists of a variety of structures, including La Harmonia store, originally built in 1920 to serve as cavalry barracks at the end of the Mexican Revolution. It is now a park concession offering food and souvenirs and has a Park Service Visitor Center on the east end where historical artifacts are displayed. Books, postcards, and other items are available at the center, and park staff will answer questions about the compound and other areas of the park. Restrooms are at the end of the parking lot.

Houses originally built as officers' quarters sit at the south and west end of the compound. Today, the houses serve as homes for concession personnel. A small museum is located in the adobe Magdalena House, where displays include photographs of biplanes used in World War I,

Cerro Castellan from Castolon

family life in the early 1900s, and pictures of La Harmonia store when it served as a major trading post.

Walk through the compound, and visit the steam engine and boiler used to move water from the Rio Grande to nearby cotton fields. Visit the reconstructed Alvino House to see what an adobe home looked like at the turn of the twentieth century. Visit the guard shack, granary, and corrals behind the store.

Don't Miss: Look at the old post office inside La Harmonia store.

Enhance Your Adventure: Pick up a copy of the twenty-page Castolon Historic District brochure printed by the National Park Service and Big Bend Natural History Association.

Follow-up to This Adventure: Buy lunch or a snack, and eat under the shade of the ramada, an arbor constructed out of river cane, outside the store.

Hunt for and Identify
Cactus at Panther Path

Starting and Ending Point: Parking area at Panther Junction Visitor Center
Time to Complete Adventure: 30 minutes to 1 hour
Distance on Foot: 50 yards
Distance in Vehicle: None
Degree of Difficulty: Easy
Preferred Time of Year: Any season
Preferred Start Time: Anytime during the day, but early morning or late afternoon is best
Age Group: All ages
Equipment Needed: 8 ounces of water per hour per person, walking shoes, hat, and sunglasses

IT might be easy to overlook the short nature trail next to the Visitor Center. At only 50 yards, the trail snakes through what looks like an ordinary piece of desert. But the thirty-five species of plants highlighted on the trail give an overview of what grows in Big Bend National Park.

Some of the plants are large and obvious, like the century plant, ocotillo, and Torrey yucca. Other small plants, like nipple cactus, would go unnoticed were it not for the marker. As you walk along the trail, take time to smell the plants. Notice the sweet smell of the huisache and the sharp smell of creosote bush. Crush a couple of leaves between your fingers, and breathe in a fragrance you will notice all over the park. Plants like sotol and lechuguilla were important to Native Americans for fiber and food. Plants like yellow trumpet and honey mesquite have always been a magnet for birds, butterflies, and mammals.

Don't Miss: Study the types of spines on various cacti. Notice that the Engelmann's prickly-pear cactus at stop #3 has 3-inch grayish spines in a cluster. Yet the blind prickly-pear at stop #24 has minute bristles, which

▲ Nipple cactus

◀ Brown-flowered cactus

you dare not touch because the bristles can embed themselves in your skin. The giant fishhook cactus at stop #9 has a long spine with a hook on the end.

Enhance Your Adventure: Purchase the nature trail brochure from the metal box at the trailhead. Read about each cactus as you walk the trail.

Follow-up to This Adventure: A visit inside the Visitor Center to see the displays and books

Explore Dugout Wells Desert Oasis

Starting and Ending Point: Parking area at Dugout Wells
Time to Complete Adventure: 1–2 hours
Distance on Foot: Minimal to 0.5 mile
Distance in Vehicle: 6 miles south of Panther Junction
Degree of Difficulty: Easy
Preferred Time of Year: Any season
Preferred Start Time: Anytime during the day, but early morning or late afternoon is best
Age Group: All ages
Equipment Needed: 8 ounces of water per hour per person, walking shoes, hat, and sunscreen

L OOK for the turnoff to Dugout Wells as you drive along the park road from the Panther Junction Visitor Center to Rio Grande Village. As you drive less than 0.25 mile down the improved dirt road, look for the trees and windmill marking the desert oasis called Dugout Wells.

In the early twentieth century, a schoolhouse at the oasis also served as a cultural hub for farmers and ranchers. The frame of the schoolhouse still stood with desks and a blackboard until the late 1930s. Today, the trees, windmill, and nature trail are the primary attractions. The working windmill squeaks and groans, pumping water to the surface as the blades turn in the wind. The well water nourishes cottonwoods, cenizo, mesquite, and a variety of desert trees, shrubs, and wildflowers. The cool, moist oasis with its trees and wildflowers draws scores of birds and butterflies, which in turn draw scores of naturalists.

Don't Miss: Walk the Chihuahuan Desert Nature Trail across from the parking area. The rock trail winds through various types of prickly-pear cacti. Many are labeled with both common and scientific names.

Windmill at Dugout Wells

Enhance Your Adventure: Carry your binoculars to spot the birds and butterflies. Photograph the Chisos Mountains with the desert in the foreground.

Follow-up to This Adventure: A visit to the nature trail at Panther Junction Visitor Center

Adventures for People with Limited Physical Mobility

Note: The following adventures may be enjoyed by anyone but are certainly attractive to those with physical limitations.

Black swallowtail

Eat While Nature Watching in the Chisos Basin

Starting and Ending Point: Chisos Mountains Lodge
Time to Complete Adventure: As long as you like
Distance on Foot: Minimal
Distance in Vehicle: Minimal
Degree of Difficulty: Easy
Preferred Time of Year: Any season
Preferred Start Time: Any meal
Age Group: All ages
Equipment needed: None, but binoculars will enhance the adventure

THE Chisos Mountains Lodge has a restaurant built in the 1960s. Three of the four walls have floor-to-ceiling windows that offer a panoramic view of the Chisos Mountains. Animals and birds at the lodge are habituated to humans and are used to going about their day-to-day business with little notice of people. Diners often leave their tables to watch a skunk amble down the walkway or to get a better look at a Say's phoebe feeding its chicks.

During the spring and summer, brilliant yellow-and-black Scott's orioles perch on low trees outside the windows. Black-chinned hummingbirds, and maybe one of the five species of other hummingbirds, feed on blooming agave, ocotillo, and penstemons. Rock squirrels, bushy critters with dark heads and brown bodies, are common along the rocks.

The restaurant offers food daily from 7:00 A.M. to 8:00 P.M., with breaks between breakfast, lunch, and dinner. Check the sign outside the restaurant for exact hours of operation.

Don't Miss: Look for birds that build nests in close proximity to the

Cactus wren

restaurant. Cactus wrens build gourd-shaped grassy nests in the cholla. Barn swallows build mud nests under the eaves of the building. Say's phoebes place their nests in the high corners on the restaurant's exterior.

Enhance Your Adventure: Ask for a table by the window so that you can get a great view of wildlife. Bring binoculars and a bird field guide or sketch pad to the dinner table.

Follow-up to This Adventure: Sunset through the Window View

Watch the Full Moon Rise over the Mountains

Starting and Ending Point: Anywhere in the park
Time to Complete Adventure: 1 hour or longer
Distance on Foot: None
Distance in Vehicle: Varied
Degree of Difficulty: Easy
Preferred Time of Year: Any month of the year, but an autumn moon appears larger than at other seasons on the horizon.
Preferred Start Time: Get into position 30 minutes before moonrise. Sometimes, dust or haze near the horizon blocks the moon. Don't give up. The wait is worth it.
Age Group: All ages
Equipment Needed: 8 ounces of water per hour per person. The temperature in the desert drops substantially at night. Wear a windbreaker during the summer and a warm jacket or coat in the other seasons to stay comfortable.

THE full moon rises in Big Bend an hour after sunset and comes over the horizon in a beautiful black sky. The night before the official full moon, moonrise occurs in a twilight sky over the horizon as the sun sets on the opposite horizon. Times can vary by an hour or more if you're in the Basin.

Don't Miss: Consult a moonrise chart to get the official time and compass direction for when and where the moon will crest the horizon. The daily weather bulletin posted by the Park Service at each Ranger Station and store gives the time for sunset and moonrise in the park. Binoculars and telescopes allow a spectacular view of the moon. Photographs of the full moon rising are best if done the night before official full moon when the sky is purple or dark blue. Pictures look better when a 300

Full moon rising above storm clouds

mm lens or larger is used. Shutter speed should be at least a 1/60 of a second. Set your camera on a tripod.

Enhance Your Adventure: Look at the moon through binoculars or telescope, and take pictures with a camera.

Follow-up to This Adventure: A drive along park roads to look for wildlife

Linger along the Window View Trail

Starting and Ending Point: Store parking lot in the Basin
Time to Complete Adventure: Less than 1 hour
Distance Traveled: 0.3 mile
Distance in Vehicle: None
Degree of Difficulty: Easy
Preferred Time of Year: Any season.
Preferred Start Time: Anytime during the day. Birds and mammals are most
  active in the early morning and late afternoon.
Age Group: All ages
Equipment Needed: 8 ounces of water per hour per person

THE concrete paved Window View Trail makes a loop around a small hill. The trail cuts through grasslands with shady areas under pine and juniper trees. Benches are placed along the trail. Access is via a gravel path behind the basin store or sidewalks with steps in front of the store and hotel. Restrooms are located at the Ranger Station next door to the basin store. A map describing points of interest along the trail is available at the trailhead for a small fee.

Don't Miss: See mammals such as Carmen white-tailed deer, javelina, and mice in the early morning and late afternoon. Roadrunner, rufous-crowned sparrow, white-winged dove, acorn woodpecker, and other birds are common. Many varieties of grass, wildflowers, and cacti grow along the trail. The vistas are spectacular any time of the day.

Enhance Your Adventure: Bring along a pair of binoculars for a better view of wildlife and plants. Stop and listen to the sounds birds make, and try to identify the birds by their calls. Carry your camera because

Greater roadrunner

there are opportunities for close-up photography and landscape photography on this short trail. This trail does not cover much distance, but it is loaded with many things to see and experience.

Follow-up to This Adventure: Rio Grande Village Nature Trail

Adventures
in a Vehicle

Sotol
Vista

Drive Ross Maxwell Scenic Drive

Starting Point: The intersection of Park Road 118 and Ross Maxwell Scenic Drive
Ending Point: Santa Elena Canyon
Time to Complete Adventure: 3–5 hours
Distance on Foot: Minimal
Distance in Vehicle: 30 miles
Degree of Difficulty: Easy
Preferred Time of Year: Any season
Preferred Start Time: Anytime during the day, but morning or afternoon is best
Age Group: 5 years to adult
Equipment Needed: 8 ounces of water per hour per person. Although this is a car trip, your body will lose moisture in the desert.

ROSS MAXWELL, the first superintendent of Big Bend National Park, began an extensive road-building campaign in 1944 that lasted until 1965. Old mining and ranch roads were redesigned to handle modern tourist traffic. In 1984, the road was officially designated the Ross Maxwell Scenic Drive.

The road takes you through some of the most spectacular and geologically interesting scenery in the park. As the road traverses a low area in the desert near Sam Nail Ranch, the full majesty of the Chisos Mountains unfolds to the east. As the road tops hills near Homer Wilson Ranch and Sotol Vista, spectacular views spread out on all sides. Then the road descends to the low desert and ends at Santa Elena Canyon. Each of the many pull-offs along the length of the road has interpretive panels with descriptions of the history and geology in the particular area. Burro Mesa Pour-off, Mule Ears Viewpoint, and Tuff Canyon Overlook have spacious parking areas. Get out of your vehicle, and take a short walk to see nearby sites.

Cerro Castellan

Don't Miss: Examine the boulders that line the parking area at Sotol Vista Overlook. Each boulder is geologically significant, but the fifth boulder from the right end has an indentation, which is a mortar where Native Americans ground grain. Farther down Ross Maxwell Scenic Drive, stop at the base of Cerro Castellan. Park in a safe spot, get out of your vehicle, and touch the ancient white volcanic ash. Look for a volcanic spine in the white ash that looks like a tree stump high up on the hillside.

Enhance Your Adventure: Buy any of the geology books for sale in the park or recommended at the end of this book.

Follow-up to This Adventure: A visit to the bookstore and gift shop at La Harmonia Store at Castolon

Four-Wheel Drive through Glenn Spring

Starting Point: 6 miles south of Panther Junction Visitor Center
Ending Point: Highway near Rio Grande Village or on highway near Castolon
Time to Complete Adventure: All day
Distance on Foot: Minimal
Distance in Vehicle: 23.5 miles
Degree of Difficulty: Four-wheel drive, high-clearance vehicle needed
Preferred Time of Year: Any season
Preferred Start Time: Early in the morning so you return by nightfall
Age Group: 7 years to adult
Equipment Needed: 64 ounces of water per person, lunch, snacks, and full tank of gas

DRIVING through the back roads of Big Bend National Park can be a white-knuckle, daring adventure but always a joy. You get a sense of the isolation as well as the primeval beauty of the land.

A drive along Glenn Spring Road offers both history and stunning scenery. Nine miles down the road, you will encounter Glenn Spring with its lovely desert willows sprouting purple tubular blooms from spring to fall. Walk along the stream and look for signs of wildlife and the remnants of an old wax factory where abundant plants called candelilla were used to make wax.

The Chisos Mountains loom large on the horizon during the first part of the drive. As the journey continues south toward the Rio Grande, the terrain changes to open desert with few bushes or cacti. The silence here is astounding.

Glenn Spring Road connects with Old River Road, a rugged and often treacherous road that is slow going at best. Turn east and you'll come out on the highway 8 miles away near Rio Grande Village. Turn west and you'll come out on the highway 43 miles away near Castolon.

Truck in the desert, Glenn Spring Road

Each route east or west has unique scenery, but choose a route based on road conditions and gasoline in your tank.

Don't Miss: Tell a park ranger what route you plan to take and when you plan to return. Park personnel do not patrol the back roads of Big Bend National Park on a regular basis; if an accident befalls you, the rangers may not find you for days unless they know you are out there.

Enhance Your Adventure: Buy *Road Guide to Backcountry Dirt Roads of Big Bend National Park* at any Ranger Station or concession in the park. Ask for other brochures about sites along Glenn Spring and Old River roads. Ensure you have the safety supplies listed in the booklets before starting your trip.

Follow-up to This Adventure: A snack at Castolon or Rio Grande Village stores

Picnic at Rio Grande Village

Starting and Ending Point: Picnic areas at Rio Grande Village
Time to Complete Adventure: 1–2 hours
Distance on Foot: Minimal
Distance in Vehicle: None
Degree of Difficulty: Easy
Preferred Time of Year: Any season
Preferred Start Time: Anytime during the day. Lunchtime is great,
    but this adventure is most suitable for breakfast or dinner.
Age Group: All ages
Equipment Needed: 8 ounces of water per hour per person, lunch,
    binoculars, and board games, deck of cards, or a good book

SEVERAL picnic areas are located at Rio Grande Village. One is under the cottonwoods adjacent to the store and restrooms. Another is at Daniels Ranch about a quarter mile west of the store. Find a picnic table and spread out your lunch. In the summer, the shade of the cottonwood trees will lower the temperature by as much as 20 degrees. In the winter, a table in the sun will warm your body like a heater.

Take a stroll around the picnic area, and watch birds in the trees. The small red bird with black wings is a vermilion flycatcher. The woodpecker with a golden head is a golden-fronted woodpecker. The large speckled bird on the ground is a roadrunner.

Don't Miss: Watch for animals in the picnic areas. If it's quiet, a bobcat or coyote might walk through on the way to a hunting location. Usually, you'll see these animals in the brush along the picnic areas. Javelinas, harmless critters despite an unsavory reputation, wander frequently through the picnic grounds at dawn or dusk.

Javelina

Enhance Your Adventure: Clean up the remnants of your picnic, and return to your car or wander over to another picnic table nearby. Sit quietly for a few minutes, and notice the birds that drop into your picnic site looking for food. We've seen turkey vultures perch on our abandoned picnic table to hunt for scraps. It's great fun to watch, but always remember: don't feed the birds and other wildlife.

Follow-up to This Adventure: A walk on the Rio Grande Village Nature Trail

Adventures
for Nature Lovers

Cottonwood
Campground
bird-watcher

Listen to the Dawn Chorus at Sam Nail Ranch

Starting and Ending Point: Parking area at Sam Nail Ranch
Time to Complete Adventure: 2–3 hours
Distance on Foot: Less than 1 mile
Distance in Vehicle: None
Degree of Difficulty: Easy
Preferred Time of Year: Any season, but spring and summer are best
Preferred Start Time: Sunrise
Age Group: 7 years to adult
Equipment Needed: 8 ounces of water per hour per person, hat, binoculars, and bird field guide

SAM and Nena Nail built a ranch on this site in the early 1900s but left the ranch when the land became a national park in 1944. A windmill stands like a ghost of the Nails, still bringing water to the surface. Birds are attracted to the water from the windmill in this parched landscape. They are also attracted to the pecan, walnut, and fig trees, where they build nests, gather insects and fruit, and seek shelter.

Dawn at Sam Nail Ranch is a magical time. Near the trailhead, birds like the cactus wren and pyrrhuloxia start singing as the sun starts to brighten the eastern sky. Black-throated sparrows, blue grosbeaks, and verdins perch on the top of mesquite trees. Farther along the trail under the thick canopy of pecan and walnut trees, watch for Bell's vireo, yellow-breasted chat, and yellow-billed cuckoo. Anywhere along the trail you will likely encounter painted and varied buntings in the spring and summer.

Don't Miss: Look for red-tailed hawks, common ravens, and turkey vultures flying overhead.

Say's phoebe

Enhance Your Adventure: Walk down the dirt road opposite the Sam Nail Ranch parking area. This road crosses open desert. Black-throated sparrows, verdins, and Say's phoebes perch on top of the yucca, mesquite, and cholla.

Follow-up to This Adventure: Lunch in the Chisos Basin and a chance to view birds that frequent the pinyon, juniper, and oak woodlands

Go on a Nighttime Owl Prowl

Starting and Ending Point: Dugout Wells, Rio Grande Village,
  or Cottonwood Campground
Time to Complete Adventure: 1 hour
Distance on Foot: Less than 1 mile
Distance in Vehicle: None
Degree of Difficulty: Easy
Preferred Time of Year: Owl prowls are productive anytime of the year but
  are best from February to July. Owls are most vocal during nesting season
  early in the year when they keep in touch with mates and fledglings.
  Summer evenings are also good times to hear owls.
Preferred Start Time: 1 hour before dusk or dawn
Age Group: 7 years to adult
Equipment Needed: 8 ounces of water per hour per person, binoculars,
  and flashlight

ANY of the wooded habitats in Big Bend National Park are home to owls. For instance, elf owls roost and nest in the cottonwoods at Dugout Wells and in holes in telephone poles at Rio Grande Village Campground. Western screech-owls roost and nest in the cottonwoods at Cottonwood Campground and at the picnic areas in Rio Grande Village.

We prefer to look for owls at Rio Grande Village because of the relative ease of spotting them in open areas at picnic grounds and campgrounds. We listen for owls immediately after sundown and discover their location based on their calls. It's not hard.

We recommend arriving at an owl location like Rio Grande Village an hour before sunset. Carry binoculars. Find a picnic table or bench where you can sit quietly and listen attentively as nighttime nature sounds replace those of daytime creatures. Owl calls can be subtle. Listen closely and stay quiet. Fidgeting and talking can produce enough noise to drown out owl calls. Once you locate an owl, train your binoculars on its profile in the dim light of dusk.

Western screech-owl

Elf owls and western screech-owls call from roosting or nesting holes at dusk and then fly to a nearby perch. Watch for the flight, and listen for the calls as the birds move to a perch. (It is illegal in the park to use flashlights or spotlights to illuminate owls or other wildlife.)

Don't Miss: Listen for owls calling to each other at the same time. Look for western screech-owls in cottonwood trees at the Rio Grande Village picnic area. We saw nearly twenty birds in a single cottonwood tree one summer evening.

Enhance Your Adventure: Listen to recorded owl calls before going on an owl prowl. It is illegal to use recordings to attract owls, so familiarize yourself with the calls ahead of time.

Follow-up to This Adventure: A drive looking for mammals and snakes along the roadways

Picnic at Cottonwood Campground

Starting and Ending Point: Cottonwood Campground
Time to Complete Adventure: 2–3 hours
Distance on Foot: Less than 0.25 mile
Distance in Vehicle: None
Degree of Difficulty: Easy
Preferred Time of Year: Any season
Preferred Start Time: Anytime during the day. Animals and birds are most active during the early morning and late afternoon.
Age Group: All ages
Equipment Needed: 8 ounces of water per hour per person, picnic lunch, snacks, and binoculars

COTTONWOOD Campground is a thirty-one-site campground located on the banks of the Rio Grande near La Harmonia store at Castolon. Rio Grande cottonwood trees shade the campground, providing a relatively comfortable setting for a picnic. The tall cottonwoods attract a variety of birds to entertain you while picnicking. If the campground is full, select a picnic table in the picnic area. If the campground has few visitors, then select a picnic table under one of the trees and unpack your picnic basket.

Stroll among the cottonwoods and along the fence lines bordering the campground to see the many birds that make the grounds one of the top destinations for birders.

Look for vermilion flycatchers, striking red birds with a black mask, perching on a low-hanging branch, a sign, a water spigot, or a barbecue grill. They'll sally out to grab insects in midair or on the ground and usually return to the same perch. Other birds, such as the golden-fronted woodpecker, western kingbird, and house finch, are common during most of the year. In spring and summer, scan the trees for nearly twenty different bird species that nest in the campground.

Wild turkey

Look for mammals like javelina and jackrabbits at the campground, and be on the lookout for a bobcat or coyote walking along the fence line in the early evening before sundown.

Don't Miss: Look at the 1,500-foot cliffs, the Sierra Ponce, opposite the campground. These cliffs are on the Mexican side of the border. Scan the cliffs with binoculars, and study the rock formations. The cliffs were exposed when the land on the U.S. side slipped down during ancient earthquakes.

Enhance Your Adventure: Bring binoculars and a spotting scope to get close-up views of birds.

Follow-up to This Adventure: A trip to La Harmonia store at Castolon or a visit to Santa Elena Canyon

Watch Dragonflies at Rio Grande Village

Starting and Ending Point: Rio Grande Village Nature Trail
Time to Complete Adventure: Less than 2 hours
Distance on Foot: Less than 1 mile
Distance in Vehicle: 24 miles from Panther Junction to Rio Grande Village
Degree of Difficulty: Easy walking on a boardwalk over a marsh and along a sandy path
Preferred Time of Year: Summer and fall
Preferred Start Time: Between 10:00 A.M. and 6:00 P.M. Dragonflies are most active during midmorning and midafternoon.
Age Group: All ages. This is a good trail for small children or family groups.
Equipment Needed: 8 ounces of water per hour per person, close-focusing binoculars, and dragonfly field guide

THE trail begins in the Rio Grande Village Campground. Walk along the path to a large pond spanned by a boardwalk. By walking slowly along the boardwalk, you can spot five or more species of dragonflies and damselflies hovering over the pond. Another four or five species may be found along the dirt path at the end of the boardwalk.

Don't Miss: Gaze out from atop the small hill at the end of the trail. The climb to the top of the hill is steep, but the view is worth the hike. Sunset over the Rio Grande is incredible from the hill's vantage point. Also, look at the small farming community across the border where people live in adobe houses and use horses and mules to plow fields— it's like looking back in time to the dawn of the twentieth century when similar farming communities existed on the U.S. side of the river.

Enhance Your Adventure: Review your field guide ahead of time. Put tabs on the pages for dragonflies or damselflies you are likely to see in Big Bend

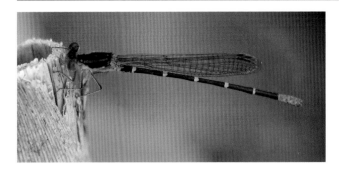

Blue-ringed dancer

Filigree skimmer

Flame skimmer dragonfly

National Park. Scan the trees at the beginning of the boardwalk and at the end of the boardwalk for perched dragonflies. Brightly colored dragonflies flying back and forth over the water are males patrolling for a female. Males usually take a break from patrolling by perching on a stick or twig in the water. Notice how the males fly off and return to the same perch.

Follow-up to This Adventure: The same activity at the Santa Elena Canyon Trail

Recommended Reading

The Big Bend: A History of the Last Texas Frontier, by Ron C. Tyler (Texas A&M University Press, 1996).

Big Bend Country: A History of Big Bend National Park, by Ross A. Maxwell (Big Bend Natural History Association, 1985).

Big Bend Country: Land of the Unexpected, by Kenneth B. Ragsdale (Texas A&M University Press, 1998).

Big Bend Landscapes, paintings and drawings by Dennis Blagg, introduction by Ron Tyler (Texas A&M University Press, 2002).

Geology of the Big Bend Area, Texas (West Texas Geological Society, Publication 72–59, 1972) (out of print but usually available from retailers specializing in "out-of-print" books).

Hiker's Guide to the Trails of Big Bend National Park, edited by John Pearson (Big Bend Natural History Association in cooperation with the National Park Service, 1990).

Hiking Big Bend National Park, by Laurence Parent (Falcon, 2005).

Lizards on the Mantel, Burros at the Door: A Big Bend Memoir, by Etta Koch with June Cooper Price (University of Texas Press, 1999).

Naturalist's Big Bend: An Introduction to the Trees and Shrubs, Wildflowers, Cacti, Mammals, Birds, Reptiles and Amphibians, Fish, and Insects, by Roland H. Wauer and C. M. Fleming (Texas A&M University Press, rev. ed., 2002).

Roadside Geology of Texas, by Darwin Spearing (Mountain Press Publishing Company, Missoula, Montana, 1991).

Who Pooped in the Park? Big Bend National Park Scat and Tracks for Kids, by Gary Robson, illustrated by Rob Rath (Farcountry Press, 2005).

Index